Introduction

The F-15 Eagle was the most famous modern jet fighter in the world during the early 1980s – bar none. Numerous toys were made of it, allowing eager youngsters such as myself to see its huge intakes, twin fins, short angular wings and shapely nose at close quarters long before we ever had the opportunity to see them in person. As such it no doubt participated in far more playground and bedroom dogfights than it ever did in real life.

That iconic aircraft with its unmistakable shape remains in service today – an incredible tribute to the engineers and designers at McDonnell Douglas who conceived it more than 50 years ago in the late 1960s. Next to the big muscular warrior that was the F-15, the F-16 seemed like a sinuous and aggressive knife-fighter and more like its unofficial 'Viper' nickname than the 'Fighting Falcon' of its official title.

These two aircraft were my introduction to the long line of exceptional aircraft that have served as fighters with the United States Air Force. When I became aware that the US had other aircraft in its inventory – thanks to books by the likes of Bill Gunston and William Green – I hit upon the idea of making my own list of USAF fighters from F-1 to F-111. This naturally proved impossible due to various gaps and the intricacies of type designation, but it also showcased the fascinating variety of aircraft that have served the USAF over the years.

When the Air Force was formed as an independent branch of the US military in 1947, the few jets that it had were all P-80/F-80 Shooting Stars. This aircraft itself was a remarkable step forward from the high-performance piston engine machines that had fought Hitler's Luftwaffe up to the end of the Second World War. Other designs soon followed, though none were quite so successful as the North American F-86 Sabre which carved out a name for itself battling MiGs over Korea.

Yet the Sabre was a dogfighter – armed with cannon and designed to get up close to the enemy before putting as many pounds of metal into it as possible until it went down. By the early 1950s it was clear t[...] of fighter combat and the [...] technology, went all-out t[...] full advantage of this new [...]

The result was a succe[...] and further away from do[...] faster, heavier and more reliant on their electronic systems than ever before. When the US became embroiled in the Vietnam War, these missile fighters struggled to match an enemy still bent on using cannon at close range. They were also found to be horribly vulnerable to advanced Soviet-made surface-to-air missile systems deployed by the North Vietnamese.

The F-4 came out of the war as the best all-round US fighter and a sales success across the free world. But lessons learned over the jungles of South-East Asia were already being fed into the design and development of America's next generation Air Force combat aircraft – the F-15 and F-16. And while dramatically upgraded versions of those aircraft remain in service today, the latest generation of fighters are yet more advanced.

When concept designs for the F-22 first became available during the early 1990s the 'stealth fighter' looked like something straight out of a science fiction film – all angles, zig-zag patterns and murky grey paint which somehow always looks 'wet'. Today the F-22 is the world's best fighter, unsurpassed by the lookalike machines coming out of China and Russia. It's new multirole sibling, the F-35, has proven controversial and it remains to be seen whether this little aircraft will fulfil its potential as a 'universal' fighter.

This publication chronicles the USAF's jet fighters through the beautiful artworks of renowned aviation illustrator JP Vieira. I hope you enjoy marvelling at the incredible variety of designs as much as I have.

Dan Sharp

ABOUT THE ARTIST

JP Vieira is an illustrator producing military history and aviation-themed artwork.

He is entirely self-taught and aims to constantly improve both the technical and artistic aspects of his work. His works combine traditional and digital methods. His attention to detail and constant pursuit of improvement makes his artworks both accurate and artistically pleasing.

JP is a published artist, collaborating with several authors, editors and publishers.

▼ **LOCKHEED-MARTIN F-22 RAPTOR**

Major Paul Lopez, F-22 Demonstration Team commander, showcases the unique capabilities of the world's premier fifth-generation fighter aircraft at the Chicago Air and Water Show, August 17, 2019. *USAF photo by 2nd Lt. Samuel Eckholm*

CONTENTS

All illustrations:
JP VIEIRA

Design:
**SEAN PHILLIPS
ATG-MEDIA.COM**

Publisher:
STEVE O'HARA

Publishing editor:
DAN SHARP

Marketing manager:
CHARLOTTE PARK

Commercial director:
NIGEL HOLE

Published by:
**MORTONS MEDIA
GROUP LTD,
MEDIA CENTRE,
MORTON WAY,
HORNCASTLE,
LINCOLNSHIRE
LN9 6JR**

Tel. **01507 529529**

Printed by:
**WILLIAM GIBBONS
AND SONS,
WOLVERHAMPTON**

MORTONS
MEDIA GROUP LTD

ISBN: 978-1-911639-09-1

044 | NORTH AMERICAN
F-100 SUPER SABRE

054 | MCDONNELL
F-101 VOODOO

060 | CONVAIR F-102
DELTA DAGGER

066 | LOCKHEED F-104
STARFIGHTER

070 | REPUBLIC F-105
THUNDERCHIEF

078 | CONVAIR F-106
DELTA DART

086 | MCDONNELL DOUGLAS
F-4 PHANTOM II

096 | GENERAL DYNAMICS
F-111 AARDVARK

098 | MCDONNELL DOUGLAS
F-15 EAGLE

108 | GENERAL DYNAMICS
F-16 FIGHTING FALCON

118 | LOCKHEED MARTIN
F-22 RAPTOR

124 | LOCKHEED MARTIN
F-35 LIGHTNING II

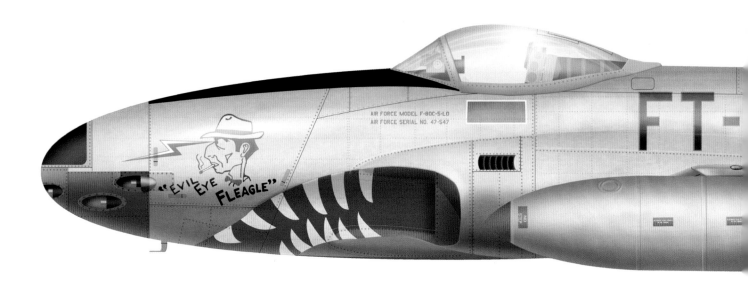

LOCKHEED F-80

Beginning its existence as the P-80 during the Second World War, the F-80 was the second American jet fighter to fly after the lacklustre Bell P-59 Airacomet. It was the first and only jet to see active service with the USAAF and was still the States' only operational jet when the USAF was formed in 1947.

Work on the XP-80 began in 1943 following the discovery that Germany was developing the twin-jet Messerschmitt Me 262. The Lockheed engineering team led by Clarence L 'Kelly' Johnson were given the task of designing a new jet fighter around the British Halford H-1B engine – later known as the de Havilland Goblin – on May 17, 1943.

Having received documents representing years of British turbojet

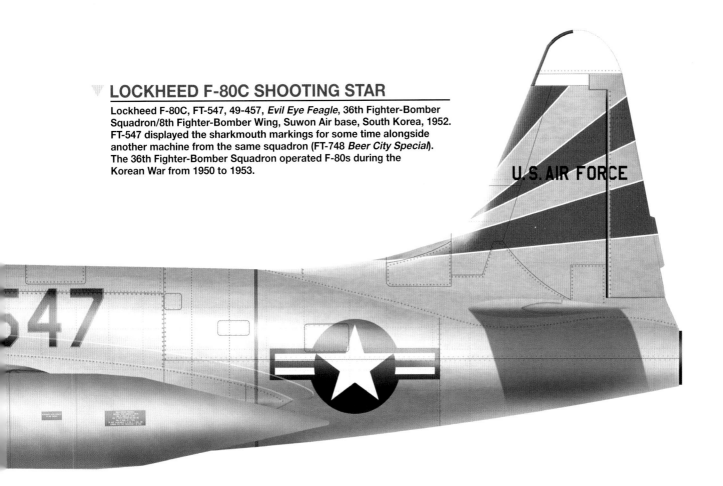

LOCKHEED F-80C SHOOTING STAR

Lockheed F-80C, FT-547, 49-457, *Evil Eye Feagle*, 36th Fighter-Bomber Squadron/8th Fighter-Bomber Wing, Suwon Air base, South Korea, 1952. FT-547 displayed the sharkmouth markings for some time alongside another machine from the same squadron (FT-748 *Beer City Special*). The 36th Fighter-Bomber Squadron operated F-80s during the Korean War from 1950 to 1953.

SHOOTING STAR

research and blueprints for the engine, Johnson put forward a design proposal the following month and estimated that the fully built prototype could be ready for testing within 180 days. In fact, it took just 143, the airframe being delivered to Muroc Army Airfield in Southern California, known today as Edwards Air Force Base, on November 16.

The first engine delivered from Britain was damaged during a ground test the following day when the aircraft's intake ducts collapsed. A replacement was urgently sought and the first XP-80, serial 44-83020, first flew on January 8, 1944. It was fitted with the last working H-1 then in existence – which had had to be removed from the prototype of the de Havilland Vampire before it could be shipped to the US.

Tests showed that the aircraft, nicknamed 'Lulu-Belle', could reach a top speed of 502mph at 20,480ft. ▶

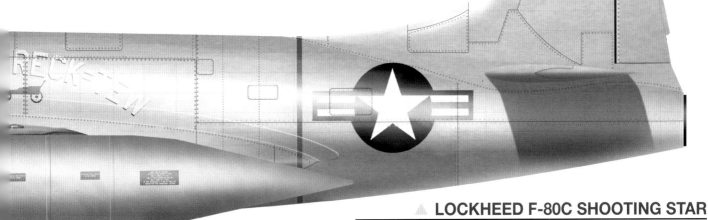

LOCKHEED F-80C SHOOTING STAR

Lockheed F-80C, FT-705, 49-705, *Ramblin' Reck Tew*, 35th Fighter Squadron, 8th Fighter-Bomber Wing, Suwon, South Korea, 1950. This aircraft achieved one of the earliest USAF jet-on-jet combat victories of the Korean War, on July 27, 1950.

Lockheed F-80 Shooting Star

▼ LOCKHEED F-80C SHOOTING STAR

Lockheed F-80C, FT-591, 4, *The Spirit of Hobo*, 80th Fighter-Bomber Squadron, 8th Fighter-Bomber Wing, Kimpo, South Korea, 1952. This aircraft, flown by 2nd Lt. Warren Guibor, was painted to mark the 50,000th sortie of the Korean War in October of 1952.

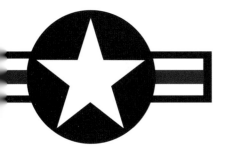

The second and third prototypes, both given the new XP-80A designation, were powered by an American development of British jet pioneer Frank Whittle's engine designs – the General Electric I-40, later built by Allison as the J-33. The first was painted in pearl grey, earning it the nickname 'Grey Ghost', while the second was left unpainted and later became known as the 'Silver Ghost'.

The 'Ghosts' were both used for engine and intake testing and while this was under way some examples of the next batch of 12 aircraft, designated YP-80A, began to enter service in late 1944. A 13th YP-80A was built and modified for photo reconnaissance but was destroyed in a crash in December 1944.

Just two pre-production YP-80A Shooting Stars saw active service during

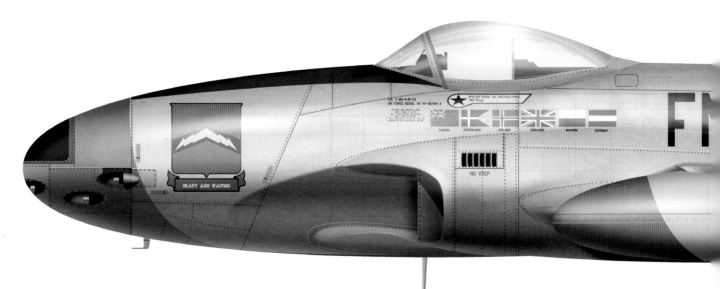

JUST TWO PRE-PRODUCTION YP-80A SHOOTING STARS SAW ACTIVE SERVICE DURING THE SECOND WORLD WAR, OPERATING BRIEFLY FROM LESINA AIRFIELD IN ITALY WITH THE 1ST FIGHTER GROUP.

LOCKHEED F-80B SHOOTING STAR

Lockheed F-80B, 16, 45-8614A, *Purrin' Kitten*, 22nd Fighter Squadron, Fürstenfeldbruck, Germany, 1948. Shown without the squadron's 'boxing bee' insignia painted on the blue disk, this aircraft had been moved to Germany with others from its unit via the Panama Canal in July 1948.

LOCKHEED F-80B SHOOTING STAR

Lockheed F-80B, FT-182, 44-85182, Aircraft Gunnery School, Nellis Air Force Base, Nevada, USA, 1950. FT-182 was used to train aircrews at the Aircraft Gunnery School, later redesignated as the USAF Fighter Weapons School and incorporating aggressor squadrons.

the Second World War, operating briefly from Lesina airfield in Italy with the 1st Fighter Group. Another two were stationed at RAF Burtonwood in Cheshire for demonstration and test flying only.

Powered by a single J-33-GE-9 jet engine mounted centrally in its fuselage, the production model Shooting Star was aerodynamically clean and was

therefore able to reach an impressive 536mph in level flight at 5000ft – though only when fully painted and without wingtip fuel tanks.

In natural metal finish and with range-extending wingtip tanks, performance tests carried out by the USAAF's Flight Test Division showed top speed to be just over 500mph – placing it behind most of its jet-powered contemporaries.

LOCKHEED F-80A SHOOTING STAR

Lockheed F-80A, FN-464, 44-85464, 56th Fighter Group, Fürstenfeldbruck, Germany, July 1948. This was the personal aircraft of the 56th Fighter Group's commander, Col. David Schilling, with special marking commemorating the conclusion of Operation Fox Able – the first USAF jet fighter crossing of the Atlantic (USA to Germany).

LOCKHEED F-80B SHOOTING STAR ▽

Lockheed F-80B, FT-043, 44-8503, 334th Fighter Squadron, Andrews AFB, USA, 1947. The 334th operated the Shooting Star for just two years, 1947 to 1949, before being re-equipped with the F-86 Sabre.

Nevertheless, the USAAF officially accepted the type into service in February 1945 and placed an initial production order for 344 P-80A examples. A further 180 followed, all of which were completed in natural metal finish and featured wingtip fuel tanks.

The next significant production model was the P-80B, which had an improved J-33 engine and, for the first time, an ejection seat – which was then retrofitted to the remaining P-80As. The P-80C had the largest production run, with 798 examples built. In addition, 129 P-80As were upgraded to P-80C spec for a total of 927 P-80Cs.

Beginning in 1948 however, all of these models would be eclipsed by the two-seater version of the design: the T-33 trainer, of which 6557 were built.

Although pilots generally enjoyed flying the P-80, redesignated F-80 in 1947, the type had its share of problems and several highly-skilled servicemen lost their lives testing early examples. Lockheed's chief engineering test pilot Milo Burcham was killed on October 20, 1944, while flying the third YP-80 from Lockheed's airfield at Burbank, California. A main fuel pump failure resulted in an engine flameout and the aircraft, which did not have an ejection seat, crashed. A newly fitted emergency fuel pump backup system might have saved his life but evidently Burcham had not been briefed on its operation.

The Grey Ghost was destroyed on March 20, 1945, when a turbine blade sheared off and tore through the aircraft's tail section, resulting in structural failure.

Burcham's replacement Tony LeVier was at the controls and managed to bail out but landed badly, breaking his back. Wearing a brace, he spent six months recovering before being able to fly again.

The highest-scoring USAAF pilot of the Second World War, Major Richard Bong, was flying a production model P-80A on August 6, 1945, when it too suffered main fuel pump failure. Evidently he forgot to activate the emergency fuel pump backup system and opted to bail out while the aircraft was inverted. Unfortunately, he was too low and his parachute failed to deploy before he hit the ground and was killed.

Both the F-80C and RF-80 photo reconnaissance version saw action during the Korean War and the F-80 was involved in both of the first jet-versus-jet kill claims. Russian MiG-15 pilot Lieutenant Semyon Fyodorovich Khominich (sometimes cited as Jominich) claimed to have shot down the F-80C of Second World War veteran Major Frank L Van Sickle Jr on November 1, 1950. The Americans claimed Van Sickle had been shot down by anti-aircraft fire. On November 8, F-80C pilot Lieutenant Russell J Brown claimed a MiG-15 destroyed – but according to Soviet records no MiGs were shot down that day.

The Korean War quickly demonstrated that the F-80 had already been superseded by the next generation of Soviet jet fighters and by the end of the war the only F-80s still operating on the front line were the RF-80s. A total of 277 F-80s were lost on active service during the Korean War – including 113 shot down by anti-aircraft fire and 14 in air-to-air combat.●

LOCKHEED F-80B SHOOTING STAR ▶

Lockheed F-80B, FT-507, USAF Fighter School, Williams Air Force base, Arizona, 1950. The first USAF jet aerobatic display team, the Acrojets, was formed from the aircraft and personnel of the fighter school in 1948.

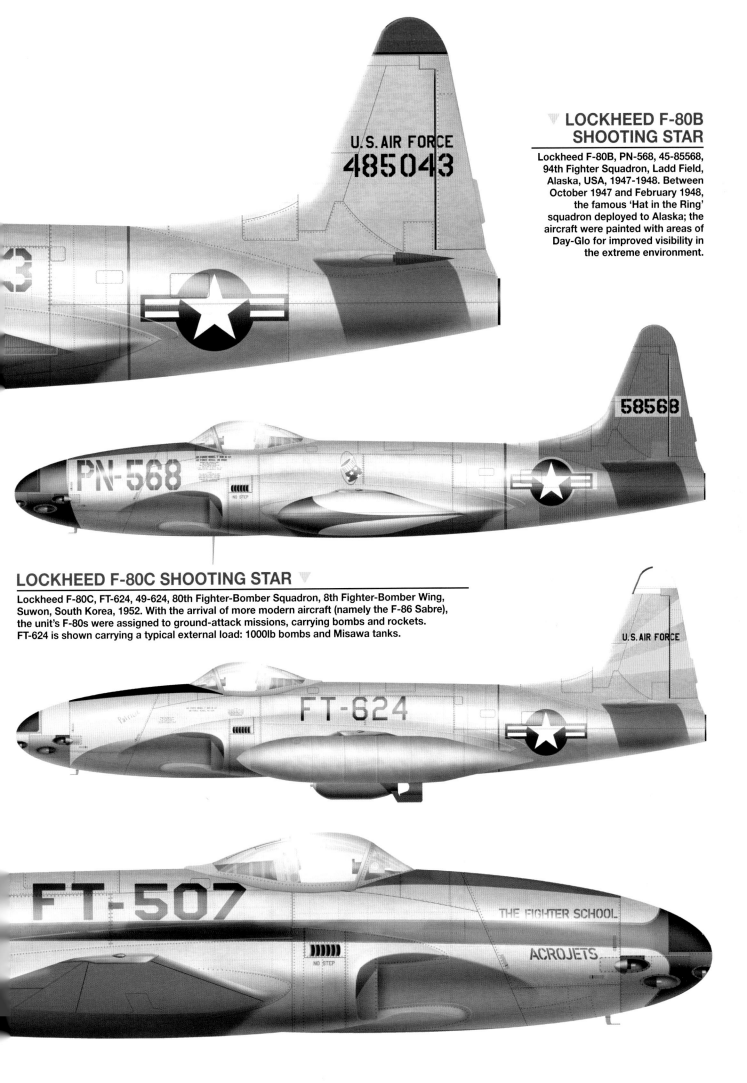

LOCKHEED F-80B SHOOTING STAR

Lockheed F-80B, PN-568, 45-85568, 94th Fighter Squadron, Ladd Field, Alaska, USA, 1947-1948. Between October 1947 and February 1948, the famous 'Hat in the Ring' squadron deployed to Alaska; the aircraft were painted with areas of Day-Glo for improved visibility in the extreme environment.

LOCKHEED F-80C SHOOTING STAR ▼

Lockheed F-80C, FT-624, 49-624, 80th Fighter-Bomber Squadron, 8th Fighter-Bomber Wing, Suwon, South Korea, 1952. With the arrival of more modern aircraft (namely the F-86 Sabre), the unit's F-80s were assigned to ground-attack missions, carrying bombs and rockets. FT-624 is shown carrying a typical external load: 1000lb bombs and Misawa tanks.

REPUBLIC F-84 THUNDERJET

Underpowered and plagued by structural and mechanical defects, the F-84 still served with distinction during the Korean War and developed into a more than adequate strike fighter.

1946-1965

▼ REPUBLIC F-84E THUNDERJET

Republic F-84E, FS-478-A, *Lil' Butch*, 51-478, 9th Fighter-Bomber Squadron, 49th Fighter Bomber Wing, Taegu Air Base (K-2), South Korea, 1952. Equipped with the JATO (Jet-Assisted Take-Off) bottles, the F-84 had a reduced take-off run and improved range and/or external load capabilities. The two bottles, one each side of the lower aft fuselage, were jettisoned after take-off and reused.

Republic Aviation was riding high on the success of its brutally powerful P-47 Thunderbolt piston-engined fighter in late 1944 when it commenced work on its first jet fighter project, designated AP-23. The development team was overseen by the company's chief designer, Alexander Kartveli, and the aircraft was designed around a single American axial-flow turbojet engine – General Electric's TG-180.

Initially it had been hoped that a turbojet version of the P-47 could be developed but this proved impractical and an entirely new design was drafted instead. After a year of development work, Republic was finally awarded a contract for three prototypes and a fourth airframe for static testing on November 11, 1945, under the designation XP-84.

The order was increased to 25 pre-production service evaluation aircraft and 75 production models on January 4, 1946, the balance later being shifted to 15 and 85 respectively. The first prototype commenced flight testing on February 28, 1946, at Muroc Air Base in California, now Edwards AFB, with Major William A Lein at the controls. It had a very simple layout – a nose intake, straight wings, a conventional tail, hydraulically actuated tricycle undercarriage and a sliding bubble canopy for the cockpit. Power came from the production version of the TG-180, the J35-GE-7 turbojet.

The fuselage was too slender to house both the engine and its fuel tanks, so the wings were made thick enough to carry the aircraft's fuel supply. In addition, the entire rear fuselage could be unbolted and removed to allow access for engine maintenance or removal. A hydraulic dive brake was installed beneath the fuselage in the centre.

The first flight of the second XP-84 took place in August 1946 and the aircraft set a new American national air speed record on September 7 at 611mph. The world record of 606.4mph set on November 7, 1945, by RAF test pilot Group Captain Hugh Joseph 'Willie' Wilson flying Gloster Meteor F.4 Britannia (EE454) was broken – but unfortunately ▶

▼ REPUBLIC F-84G-20-RE THUNDERJET

Republic F-84G-20-RE, FS-240, 51-1240, 49th Fighter-Bomber Group, 1954. This aircraft is equipped with in-flight refuelling (IFR) probes on the wingtip tanks. This was the first IFR method (probe and drogue) used operationally by the USAF. Introduced with the F-84E, the system was continued into the G-series before being replaced with the boom and receptacle system – the receptacle being located on the left wing. During Operation High Tide in May 1952, 12 F-84Es used IFR to fly non-stop from Japan to attack targets located in North Korea. That same year Operation Fox Peter saw F-84 units flying non-stop across the Pacific using IFR.

Republic F-84 Thunderjet

▲ REPUBLIC F-84G THUNDERJET

Republic F-84G, FS-966, 51-966, 77th Fighter-Bomber Squadron, 20th Fighter-Bomber Group, RAF Wethersfield, UK, 1952. The F-84G was the first fighter able to deliver a nuclear bomb – carrying a single Mk.7 bomb on its left wing pylon. The 20th Fighter-Bomber Wing, including the 55th, 77th and 79th FBS, was stationed in the UK in 1952, allowing the USAF to field nuclear-equipped jet fighters close to the potential European/USSR front line.

for the XP-84 another Gloster Meteor F.4 pilot, Group Captain Edward 'Teddy' Mortlock Donaldson, managed to achieve 615.78mph that same day.

General Electric was struggling with the J35-GE-7 so the third prototype, designated XP-84A, was powered by the Allison-built J35-A-15. This would serve as the template for the 15 pre-production

XP-84A service evaluation aircraft – although these were also fitted with four nose-mounted 0.50-calibre M2 Browning machine guns and another one in each of their wing roots. They could also be equipped with wingtip tanks, each holding 230 US gallons.

The full production version was the P-84B, which had a slightly improved

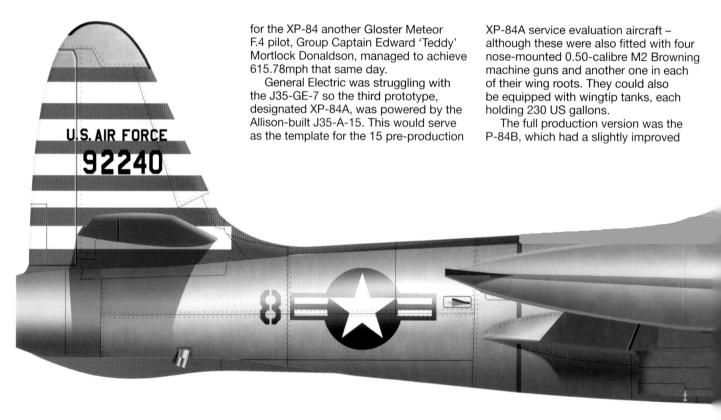

REPUBLIC F-84E THUNDERJET ▲

Republic F-84E, FS-240, 49-2240, 527th Fighter-Bomber Squadron, 86th Fighter-Bomber Wing, Neubiberg AB, West Germany, 1952. This aircraft features the early unframed canopy fitted to all models until the G variant. The framed canopy was later retrofitted to earlier variants.

REPUBLIC F-84E THUNDERJET ▶

Republic F-84E, FS-493, 51-493, 523rd Fighter-Escort Squadron, 27th Fighter-Escort Group, 1951. 1st Lt. Jacob Kratt would become the F-84's highest scoring Korean War pilot when he downed a Yak-3 on January 26, 1951, following on from a double MiG-15 kill achieved three days earlier.

REPUBLIC F-84E THUNDERJET

Republic F-84E, FS-648, 51-648, 525th Fighter-Bomber Squadron, 86th Fighter-Bomber Group, Neubiberg AB, West Germany, 1952. The group commander's aircraft, it displays the colours of the group's three squadrons: blue for the 525th FBS, red for the 526th FBS and yellow for the 527th. Commander's aircraft were typically the most visually striking on the flightline.

engine, M3 machine guns and an ejection seat – although the latter was never approved for use. The type entered service with the 14th Fighter Group in December 1947 and it was quickly found to have serious problems. It had the power to go faster than Mach 0.8 but above that speed at low altitude it could suffer from control reversal and

sudden violent pitch-up which could cause its wings to snap off. Above 15,000ft it was possible to fly faster but only with severe buffeting.

If an acceleration load greater than 5.5 g was applied, the aircraft's skin wrinkled too. Nevertheless, most YP-84As would later be brought up to P-84B standard and a total of 226 P-84Bs were delivered ▶

Republic F-84 Thunderjet

to the air force between August 1947 and February 1948.

The entire P-84B fleet was grounded on May 24, 1948, following a series of structural failures. The P-84C, similar to the 'B' but with an improved electrical system and engine, began production in May 1948 and the type was then redesignated F-84 on June 11, 1948.

Neither the 'B' nor the 'C' proved to be reliable and even before the structural problems became apparent both suffered had from a number of mechanical issues which frequently made them unserviceable. These included problems with the undercarriage hydraulics, a cramped and uncomfortable cockpit and a lack of engine power.

These deficiencies prompted the USAF to seriously consider cancelling the F-84 and Republic was put under pressure to bring the aircraft up to scratch. This resulted in the 'quick fix'

interim F-84D, which brought together a wide range of amendments in an attempt to cure the worst of the type's failings before the introduction of a completely redesigned version – the F-84E.

Among the F-84D's upgrades were a substantially more powerful engine – the Allison J35-A-17D – mechanically rather than hydraulically actuated landing gear, stronger wings, thicker aluminium skin, wingtip tank fins to prevent flexing, a winterised fuel system, a usable ejection seat and a quick-release cockpit canopy. A total of 154 F-84Ds were delivered between November 1948 and April 1949.

The first F-84E made its initial flight on May 18, 1949, and incorporated further wing reinforcement, a radar gunsight, provision for rocket-assisted take-off, a 12in longer fuselage forward of the wings, resulting in a more comfortable cockpit, and a 3in extension aft of the wings to expand the avionics bay. It also had ▶

REPUBLIC F-84G THUNDERJET ▽

Republic F-84G, 51-16719, 3600th Air demonstration Team (USAF Thunderbirds), Luke AFB, 1954.
The Thunderjet was the first aircraft used by the famous Thunderbirds display team, who flew
the aircraft from 1953 to 1955.

REPUBLIC F-84G THUNDERJET

Republic F-84G, FS-821-A, 51-821, 31st Fighter-Escort Wing Turner AFB, Georgia, 1952. Although several other external weapons configurations were tested, including replacing the wingtip tanks with rocket assemblies, the one depicted here was commonly used operationally, allowing for a balance between offensive capability and range.

THE LAST STRAIGHT-WING VARIANT WAS THE F-84G, WHICH ENTERED SERVICE IN 1951 AS A STOPGAP NUCLEAR STRIKE FIGHTER AHEAD OF THE INTRODUCTION OF THE SWEPT-WING F-84F.

REPUBLIC F-84G THUNDERJET

Republic F-84G, FS-273, 508th Strategic Fighter Wing, Turner Air Force Base, Georgia 1954. The 508th SFW carried out long range missions, from bomber escort to air defence, and was frequently deployed abroad to Europe and the Far East. In-flight refuelling was performed by KC-97 tankers.

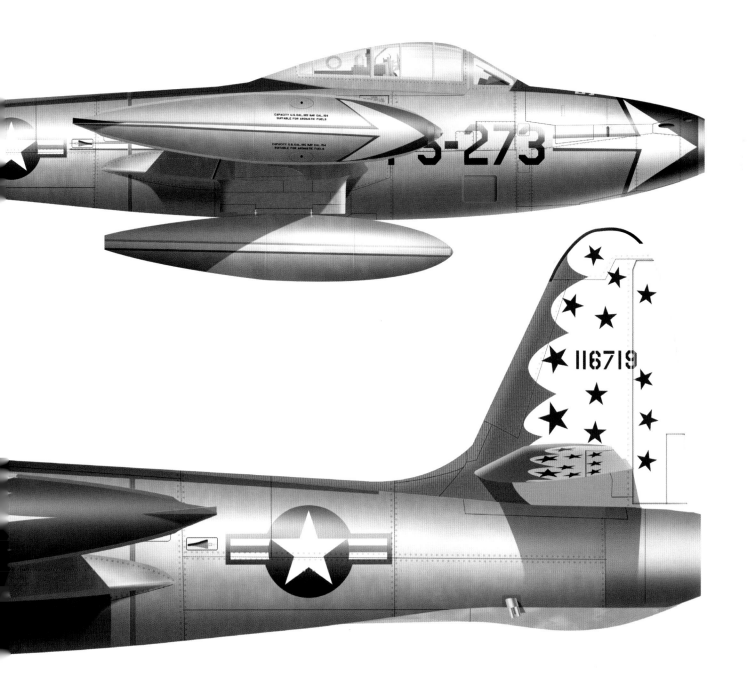

Republic F-84 Thunderjet

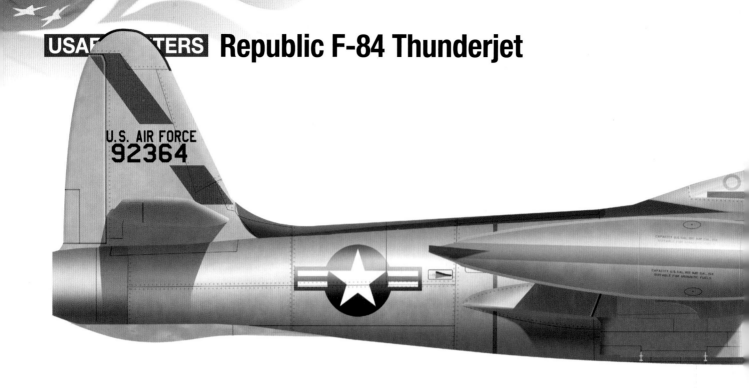

U.S. AIR FORCE
92364

REPUBLIC F-84E ▷ THUNDERJET

Republic F-84G, FS-454, 51-10454, *Four Queens*, **430th Fighter-Bomber Squadron, 474th Fighter-Bomber Wing, Taegu AB, South Korea, 1953.** FS-454 was the aircraft of the 474th's commander Col. Joseph Davis Jr. At the end of the Korean War, Davis was the commander of all F-84 units in theatre. The aircraft displays all the colours of the units assigned to the 474th: red for the 428th FBS; blue for the 429th FBS and yellow for the 430th FBS.

rocket racks which folded flat against the wing once their rockets had been fired.

Between May 1949 and July 1951, 843 F-84Es were built and many saw action during the Korean War. However, the F-84 proved inferior to the MiG-15 and during early combat operations 18 Thunderjets were lost compared to nine MiGs. In one instance, an F-84E pilot intentionally made use of the type's tendency to violently pitch up above Mach 0.8 at low altitude – the MiGs following him were unable to match the manoeuvre and one of them crashed into the ground.

Heavily loaded for combat operations, particularly in hot weather, the F-84 proved difficult to get airborne and quickly earned the nicknames 'lead sled' and 'hog' due to its 'love of the ground'.

When the F-86 joined the war, the F-84 replaced the F-80 as the USAF's in-theatre strike fighter. The last straight-

wing variant was the F-84G, which entered service in 1951 as a stopgap nuclear strike fighter ahead of the introduction of the swept-wing F-84F. It featured a more powerful J35-A-29, framed canopy, refuelling boom, autopilot, instrument landing system and option to carry a single Mark 7 nuclear bomb. The USAF display team, the Thunderbirds, operated F-84Gs from 1953 to 1955.

Despite all the improvements made to the F-84, serviceability remained poor during the Korean War primarily due to a lack of spares from Allison for the J35. The F-84B and C had both been withdrawn from service by the end of 1952 while the F-84D continued in Air National Guard service until 1957. The F-84E ended its days with the USAF in 1956 but continued on with the ANG until 1959 and the F-84G was retired from air force service during the mid-1960s.●

REPUBLIC F-84E THUNDERJET

Republic F-84E, FS-364, 49-2364, 524th Fighter-Escort Squadron, 27th Fighter-Escort Wing, Taegu AB, South Korea, 1951. The 27th FEW was forward deployed to the Far East when the Korean War began, operating from both Japan and South Korea. It was the first F-84 unit to see combat and also the first to achieve a confirmed MiG kill.

REPUBLIC F-84G THUNDERJET

Republic F-84G, FS-669, 51-1669, Skyblazers demonstration team, 492nd Fighter-Bomber Squadron, 48th Fighter-Bomber Wing, Chaumont AB, France, 1953. The Skyblazers were formed in 1949 with pilots and F-80s from the 22nd Fighter Squadron (36th Fighter Wing) based in Fürstenfeldbruk, West Germany. They switched to flying F-84s in 1950.

REPUBLIC F-84F THUNDER

1950–1972

Conceived as a swept-wing Thunderjet, the F-84F Thunderstreak ended up sharing few components with its predecessor. What both types had in common, however, was unreliability and mechanical difficulties.

With production of the F-84E well under way, Republic decided to see whether applying German Second World War swept-wing research to the design would result in a significant increased in performance. The company used its own funding to design the AP-23M and rebuild the 409th F-84E off the production line with 40⁰ swept-back wings.

It also had a J35-A-25 engine with 5200lb-ft of thrust – compared

REPUBLIC F-84F-25-RE THUNDERSTREAK

Republic F-84F-25-RE Thunderstreak, FS-734, 51-1734, 390th Fighter-Bomber Squadron, 366th Fighter-Bomber Wing, Alexandria AFB (later, England AFB), Louisiana, 1956. The Wild Boars flew Thunderstreaks during two separate periods: from 1954 to 1958 at Alexandria AFB and then again from 1962-1965 based at Chambley AB, France, and later at Holloman Air Force Base, New Mexico.

STREAK

to the J35-A-17D of the standard 'E' which developed 5000lb – and its windscreen was redesigned to improve its aerodynamic profile too. Equipped with the new wings, the aircraft made its first flight on June 3, 1950, and during one early low-altitude test managed to achieve a very respectable 693mph.

The type was initially designated YF-96A but the USAF showed little interest. This attitude changed with the appearance of MiG-15s over Korea and

Republic was awarded a development contract in July 1950. The air force required the company to fit the type with a Curtiss-Wright J65 engine – a licence-built copy of the British Armstrong Siddeley Sapphire – and two months later the type was redesignated F-84F but given a new official nickname, Thunderstreak, to differentiate it from the straight-winged F-84.

Rather than carve up another F-84 to fit the new engine, Republic simply

REPUBLIC F-84F-35-RE THUNDERSTREAK

Republic F-84F-35-RE Thunderstreak, FS-454, 52-6454, 511th Fighter-Bomber Squadron, 405th Fighter-Bomber Wing, Langley AFB, Virginia, 1955. The 405th FBW was the first Tactical Air Command unit to begin conversion to the Thunderstreak in 1954.

Republic F-84F Thunderstreak

REPUBLIC F-84F-25-RE THUNDERSTREAK ▷

Republic F-84F-25-RE Thunderstreak, FS-657, 51-1657, 366th Tactical Fighter Wing, Chaumont-Semoutiers Air Base, France, 1962. Alongside the 12th TFW and 15th TFW, the 366th was one of the units set up by the USAF using aircraft and personnel from former ANG units when the Thunderstreak was reactivated.

▽ REPUBLIC F-84F-50-RE THUNDERSTREAK

Republic F-84F-50-RE Thunderstreak, FS-852, 52-6852, 91st Fighter-Bomber Squadron, 81st Fighter-Bomber Wing, RAF Bentwaters, UK, 1955. The 81st FBW was based at the UK and its aircraft displayed a nuclear mushroom insignia on the fuselage port side.

REPUBLIC F-84F-40-GE THUNDERSTREAK ▲

Republic F-84F-40-GE Thunderstreak, FS-578, 52-6578, 12th Strategic-Fighter Wing, Bergstrom AFB, Texas 1953. Displaying the wing's commanders colours, this Thunderstreak belongs to the 12th SFW, which was tasked with escorting SAC bombers.

altered the single existing YF-96A aircraft, turning it into the YF-84F by deepening its fuselage and enlarging its nose intake. And it flew for the first time with this new powerplant on February 14, 1951. Two purpose-built YF-84Fs prototypes followed – one of which featured a completely new intake configuration: a solid nose and intakes in its wingroots.

It had been hoped that the F-84F would enter full series production during the autumn of 1951 but it proved difficult to manufacture the type's wings, requiring a redesign, and there were also issues with the engine installation. As a result, it was decided that the straight-winged F-84G would enter production as a stopgap measure until the F-84F was ready. This was a wise move since the first production model F-84F did not make its first flight until November 22, 1952.

In addition to its new wings, engine and fuselage, the aircraft also differed from the straight-winged F-84 in having a one-piece flip-up cockpit canopy where the Thunderjet's slid to the rear; a pair of air brakes on the sides of the rear fuselage rather than a single brake under the fuselage; powered flight controls; leading edge slats and a spine running down the back of its fuselage.

The F-84F retained the F-84E's six Browning M3 machine guns and had four underwing pylons for carrying stores. The F-84F's swept wings could not take wingtip tanks so the inner pylons were designed to carry external fuel tanks and the 'F' could also deliver a nuclear bomb using the LABS mechanism.

Although the J65-W-1 engine was fitted to the first 275 Thunderstreaks, this was replaced with the J65-W-1A for the next 100 and thereafter aircraft rolling off the production line. Neither powerplant was very reliable and aircraft fitted with them could not later be re-engined with ▶

USAF FIGHTERS Republic F-84F Thunderstreak

more reliable designs – meaning their service lifespan was limited.

After the first 375 F-84Fs, the somewhat more reliable J65-W-3 and J65-B-3 (manufactured by Buick) were introduced, each providing 7220lb-ft of thrust. Even so, the aircraft had a high landing speed and although it was faster than the straight-winged F-84s it did not handle well near its limit. These problems prompted Republic to suspend production in 1954 and reassess the F-84F's design. When production restarted in 1955, the new aircraft were fitted with 'all-moving' tailplanes – preventing a tendency to pitch-up during a high-speed stall.

The whole fleet was grounded in 1955 due to repeated engine failures. Improvements were made but the J65 could not be raised to a satisfactory standard and the USAF began to phase the F-84F out of active service that year. The phaseout was completed by 1958 with remaining aircraft being relegated to Air National Guard units. However, the fleet was reactivated in 1961 due to tensions in Germany as the Berlin Wall was constructed. Control rod corrosion led to the fleet being grounded yet again in 1962 and structural corrosion eventually forced the retirement of all F-84Fs in 1971.

Overall, 2711 F-84F Thunderstreaks, including prototypes, had been manufactured by August 1957. However, only 1410 of these served with the USAF, the remainder being sent to American allies including Belgium, France, West Germany, Greece, Italy, Holland and Turkey.

Having arrived too late to see service during the Korean War, no American Thunderstreaks saw combat – although French F-84s were used to attack Egyptian positions during the Suez Crisis in 1956 and two Turkish F-84Fs shot down two Iraqi Ilyushin Il-28 Beagle bombers that had entered Turkish airspace on August 16, 1962.

The second YF-84F prototype, with the solid nose and wing root intakes, became the basis for the RF-84F Thunderflash reconnaissance aircraft. The first full production model RF-84F was delivered in 1953 but the type was delayed by the same difficulties which afflicted the F-84F programme and it did not become fully active in USAF service until 1955.

Like the straight-winged F-84s the F-84F was seen as a passable fighter-bomber but suffered from design flaws and was dogged by constant reliability issues.●

REPUBLIC F-84F-35-RE THUNDERSTREAK ▷

Republic F-84F-35-RE Thunderstreak, FS-500, 52-6500, 509th Fighter-Bomber Squadron, 405th Fighter-Bomber Wing, 1954. FS-500 is seen carrying a practice Mk.7 nuclear bomb on the port inner pylon and a total of three external fuel tanks.

REPUBLIC F-84F-45-RE THUNDERSTREAK ▷

Republic F-84F-45-RE Thunderstreak, 52-6751, 6751, USAF 3600th Air Demonstration Team Thunderbirds, Luke AFB, Arizona, 1955. The Thunderstreak was the second aircraft type to be used by the Thunderbirds, from 1955 to 1956.

REPUBLIC F-84F-45-RE THUNDERSTREAK

Republic F-84F-45-RE Thunderstreak, FS-737, 52-6737, 92nd Fighter-Bomber Squadron, 81st Fighter-Bomber Wing, RAF Manston UK, 1955. Another component squadron of the UK-based 81st FBW, the 92nd FBS transitioned to the F-84F in 1954.

26737

FS-737

26500

U.S. AIR FORCE

MISANTHROPIC MARY

U.S. AIR FORCE

NORTH AMERICAN F-86A, E, F AND H SABRE

1947-1958

Standing head and shoulders above all the other American jets of the 1950s, the F-86 became a legend in its own time – fighting MiG-15s above the war-torn Korean peninsula. Today it remains an icon of the early jet age.

NORTH AMERICAN F-86F-1-NA SABRE

North American F-86F-1-NA Sabre, FU-910, 51-2910, *Beauteous Butch II*, 39th Fighter-Interceptor Squadron, 51st Fighter-interceptor Wing, Suwon Air Base (K13), South Korea, 1953. With 16 aerial victories and five more enemy aircraft damaged, Captain Joseph C. McConnell Jr. was the leading American ace of the Korean War. This image represents his aircraft after it was painted for publicity photos – the victory markings were repainted as red stars rather than MiG silhouettes – and the name was repainted as *Beauteous Butch II* rather than *Beautious Butch II* as it was originally.

The US Navy drew up a requirement for a jet-powered shipboard fighter during the autumn of 1944 and North American, builder of one of the USAAF's most advanced and capable fighters – the P-51 Mustang – responded with project NA-134. The underwhelming result was the FJ-1 Fury, a single engine aircraft with a nose intake plus wings, tail surfaces and a cockpit canopy which owed much to those of the Mustang.

The earliest known drawing of the NA-134 is dated October 13, 1944, and just over five weeks later, the USAAF issued a requirement for a medium-range day fighter with a top speed of 600mph. North American revisited the NA-134 design and amended it to incorporate a slimmer fuselage and a revised wing form. It was to have six 0.5in machine guns in its nose – three on either side of the intake. This became the NA-140 and North American received a contract for three prototypes under the designation XP-86 in May 1945.

With the end of the Second World War in Europe that month, a considerable quantity of German aerodynamics test data and research material fell into American hands. Like every other US defence contractor, North American had full access to this valuable information and quickly realised its potential.

A swept-wing for the XP-86 was first discussed in June 1945 and following a host of wind tunnel tests the design's original straight wing was scrapped. Work began in earnest on a new swept

wing. A final wing form had been chosen by October 1946 and on December 20 North American received a contract for 33 full production model P-86As and 190 P-86Bs.

The P-86B, based on North American model NA-152, had larger mainwheels and bigger brakes than the 'A', a correspondingly wider fuselage, increased tail area, improved internal fuel capacity, gun heating and a canopy ejection system.

It was cancelled in September 1947, however, when it became clear that small high-pressure tyres and advances in braking technology made the 'B' superfluous. Another 188 F-86As were ordered instead.

Less than a month later, on October 1, 1947, the first prototype XP-86 made its flight debut. It was found that the type lacked sufficient power from its Allison J35 engine and there were issues with its landing gear which meant the aircraft had to be flown with the gear locked in the down position. In addition, it was found that it could become unstable at high speeds due to its elevator assembly. As the aircraft got closer to the speed of sound a shock wave formed on the elevator's hinge line and the result was ineffective control surfaces.

Top speed was just over 510mph. After two months of company tests, the first XP-86 was handed over to the USAF – as it now was – for the second phase of its test regime. This lasted just six days, after which the air force's test pilot Major Ken Chilstrom declared that the USAF now had the best jet fighter developed up to that date anywhere in the world. North American then received a production contract for a further 225 P-86As.

Also in December 1947, the air force ordered two prototypes of the NA-157, designated P-86C. This was to be a ▶

NORTH AMERICAN F-86A-5-NA SABRE

North American F-86A-5-NA Sabre, FU-318, 49-1318, 334th Fighter-Interceptor Squadron, 4th Fighter-Interceptor Wing, Suwon Air Base (K13), South Korea, 1951. Captain James Jabara was the world's first jet-versus-jet ace, achieving his fifth and sixth MiG-15 kills on May 20, 1951. This is the aircraft flown by Jabara on that day. He ended the war with 15 kills, after two tours in Korea and flying several different aircraft.

NORTH AMERICAN F-86F-1-NA SABRE

North American F-86F-1-NA Sabre, FU-857, 51-2857, 334th Fighter-Interceptor Squadron, 4th Fighter-Interceptor Wing, Kimpo AB (K-14), South Korea, 1953. The image shows Capt. 'Pete' Fernandez's aircraft on May 1953; markings include three stars below the ground crew's names, as kills awarded to them. Fernandez finished the Korean War with 14.5 kills.

North American F-86A, E, F and H Sabre

NORTH AMERICAN F-86A-5-NA SABRE

North American F-86A-5-NA Sabre, 49-1175, FU-175, *Peg O' My Heart*, 336th Fighter-Interceptor Squadron, 4th Fighter-Interceptor Wing, Kimpo AB (K-14), South Korea, 1952. One of the most colorful machines of the Rocketeers, *Peg O' My heart*, sported a shark mouth, a feature not often seen until later on the conflict.

long-range fighter with a solid nose and side intakes but it proved so different from the original series that it was later redesignated YF-93A.

The P-86A differed from the three prototypes in having the much more powerful General Electric J47 engine and a redesigned nosewheel door to cure the earlier undercarriage issue. The openings for the aircraft's six cannon on the sides of the nose were covered with panels which opened automatically when they were fired and closed again afterwards. Numerous internal changes refined the

cockpit design and systems layout.

In the air, the P-86A's official top speed was 585mph – making it more than 70mph faster than the prototypes. From June 1, 1948, the P-86A became the F-86A. The first deliveries to an active service unit were made on February 14, 1949, to the 1st Maintenance Support Group of the 1st Fighter Group.

At around the same time, the USAF issued a requirement for a new radar-equipped interceptor and on March 28, 1949, North American put forward project NA-164. This single seater, which became

the F-86D, is discussed separately elsewhere in this publication.

Even as the F-86A was entering service, North American was investigating ways of preventing the loss of elevator control at high speeds identified during the XP-86 flight tests. An extension of the trailing edge had alleviated the problem sufficiently for the F-86A but had not cured it entirely.

The answer proved to be an 'all-moving tail' where the entire tailplane assembly operated as a moveable control surface. Work on designing an F-86 with

NORTH AMERICAN F-86F-30-NA SABRE

North American F-86F-30-NA Sabre, 52-4371, FU-371, 67th Fighter-Bomber Squadron, Osan Air Base, South Korea, 1953. The Fighting Cocks were re-equipped with Sabres in 1953. It is shown carrying a bomb on its internal wing pylon, representative of the use of the Sabre in air-to-ground missions. After the Korean War the squadron remained in the East Asian region, deploying frequently from South Korea to Japan, Taiwan and the Philippines.

> IN THE AIR, THE P-86A'S OFFICIAL TOP SPEED WAS 585MPH – MAKING IT MORE THAN 70MPH FASTER THAN THE PROTOTYPES. FROM JUNE 1, 1948, THE P-86A BECAME THE F-86A.

NORTH AMERICAN F-86E-10-NA SABRE

North American F-86E-10-NA Sabre, 51-2746, FU-746, *Michigan Center / Lady Frances*, 51st Fighter-Interceptor Wing, Suwon Air Base (K-13), South Korea, 1952. A Second World War ace with 28 kills, Col. Francis 'Gabby' Gabreski continued his career in Korea, achieving six and a half kills in Sabres. He first flew with the 4th FIW and then commanded the 51st FIW. This was his aircraft during much of the later period, marked as *Lady Frances* (on the port side), but it was also used by Maj. William H. Wescott, another Korean War ace with five kills.

NORTH AMERICAN F-86F-30-NA SABRE

North American F-86F-30-NA Sabre, 52-4877, FU-877, *Miss Tena*, 8th Fighter-Bomber Wing, Suwon Air Base (K-13), South Korea, 1953. This Sabre is the wing's commander aircraft and displays the colours of all three component squadrons: blue for the 35th Fighter-Bomber Squadron (FBS), red for the 36th FBS and yellow for the 80th FBS.

this feature began on November 15, 1949, with the designation NA-170. The USAF then awarded North American a contract for 111 examples of the aircraft as the F-86E on January 17, 1950.

The aircraft also included a new hydraulic system which prevented external loads on the control surfaces from being transferred to the pilot's control stick. Instead, preloaded springs were used to provide the pilot with a simulation of 'feel' when moving the stick. The first 'E' took to the air on September 23, 1950, and the first deliveries to the air force took place

in February 1951. A total of 456 F-86Es were made.

The definitive F-86 day fighter appeared in the form of the F-86F – with work on the new version commencing on July 31, 1950, as the NA-172. The main difference between the 'E' and the 'F' was the installation of the much improved J47-GE-27 engine. It was also fitted with a gunsight-mounted gun camera and had provision to carry AN-M10 chemical tanks on its external pylons.

A contract for 109 F-86Fs placed in April 1951 was increased to 360 examples on June 30.

NORTH AMERICAN F-86E-5-NA SABRE

North American F-86E-5-NA Sabre, 50-648, FU-648, *Eight Ball Express / Pretty Mary*, 336th Fighter-Interceptor Squadron, 4th Fighter-Interceptor Wing, Kimpo Air Base (K-13), South Korea, 1952. *Eight Ball Express* was flown by several pilots in both the 334th FIS and 336th FIS during the conflict and afterwards was assigned to the 35th FBS, based in Japan.

North American F-86A, E, F and H Sabre

NORTH AMERICAN F-86F-25-NA SABRE ▲

North American F-86F-25-NA Sabre, 52-5333, FU-333, 461st Fighter-Day Squadron, 36th Fighter-Day Group, Landstuhl Air Base, West Germany, 1956. Wearing a colour scheme of Sea Grey and Dark Green, this Sabre was used in a series of camouflage tests. This camouflage was not adopted into service however and Sabres in USAF service almost invariably had a metal finish.

▲ NORTH AMERICAN F-86F-30-NA SABRE

North American F-86F-30-NA Sabre, 52-4656, FU-656, 417th Fighter-Bomber Squadron, 50th Fighter-Bomber Group, Hahn Air Base, West Germany, 1954. The 417th FBS was deployed to West Germany in 1953, during Operation Fox Able 20, reinforcing USAF units in Europe.

NORTH AMERICAN F-86A-5-NA SABRE ▲

North American F-86A-5-NA Sabre, 49-1262, FU-262, 94th Fighter-Interceptor Squadron, 1st Fighter-Interceptor Group, George Air Force Base, California, 1953. The famous Hat in the Ring squadron was assigned to the 1st FIG, providing air defence for the Western Continental USA. It flew Sabres from 1954 to 1956 before transitioning to F-100 Super Sabres.

Before this, however, North American had begun work on a pure fighter-bomber version of the F-86 under project number NA-187. It was to be fitted with the powerful General Electric J73 and this required not only a larger intake at the front of the aircraft but also a 6in deeper fuselage. A beneficial side-effect of this increase in fuselage space was additional internal fuel tank capacity – from 435 gallons up to 562.

A clamshell cockpit canopy and ejection seat similar to those of the F-86D were fitted – though both items were unique to the NA-187 design. Tail surfaces were of increased area and of the single piece 'all-moving' type. A mock-up was ready for inspection on July 24 but the USAF did not immediately order it into production.

Deliveries of the F-86F to the 126th Fighter-Interceptor Squadron had commenced on April 1, 1952, and throughout that month most new F-86Fs were allocated to units operating in Korea. Two months later the 'F' was upgraded as the F-86F-5. This could carry either standard 120 gallon drop tanks or new 200 gallon tanks and the electrical system was also improved. The F-86F-10 quickly followed, introducing a new gunsight.

Meanwhile, North American had commenced yet another F-86 based project, NA-191, on October 26, 1951, which consisted of an otherwise standard F-86F capable of carrying two under-wing stores instead of just one – effectively turning the aircraft into a fighter-bomber. The first of these upgraded F-86s began rolling off the company's Inglewood production lines during October 1952.

The NA-187 pure fighter-bomber was finally ordered, as the F-86H, on November 3, 1952. At the same time,

NORTH AMERICAN F-86A-5-NA SABRE

North American F-86A-5-NA Sabre, 49-1261, FU-261, 91st Fighter-Interceptor Squadron, 81st Fighter-Interceptor Wing, RAF Bentwaters Air Base, UK, 1951. The 91st FIS was part of the USAFE, tasked with reinforcing the UK's air defence.

NORTH AMERICAN F-86A-5-NA SABRE

North American F-86A-5-NA Sabre, 49-1306, FU-306, 27th Fighter-Interceptor Squadron, 1st Fighter Group, Griffiss Air Force Base, New York, 1951. The 27th Squadron was assigned to the 1st FIG, providing air defence for the Eastern Continental USA. It flew F-86As from 1949 to 1954.

North American was working on an improved version of the F-86F's wing. This had a 6in leading edge extension at the root and 3in at the wingtip (it was referred to as the '6-3' wing), meaning that overall wing area was increased from 287.9sq ft to 302.3sq ft. At the same time, the automatic slats that had been a feature of earlier F-86s were deleted. Airflow across the wing was reduced with the introduction of 5in tall wing fences.

Maximum speed of the '6-3' winged F-86F was increased to 608mph at 35,000ft compared to the standard F-86F's 604mph. Unfortunately, the

stall speed also changed, from 128mph to 144mph and the stall became more difficult to manage with increased yaw and roll. A total of 50 '6-3' wing kits were transported to Korea so that F-86Fs serving with operational units could be upgraded.

The first prototype F-86H flew on April 30, 1953, and starting with the second prototype the F-86H was able to carry a Mk 12 20-kiloton nuclear bomb – dropped using an M-1 LABS (Low Altitude Bombing System) computer. Deliveries commenced on August 2, 1954, and the type began to enter

service with operational units starting in November 1954.

The F-86F continued in USAF service after the Korean War but the majority of airframes were phased out in 1955. A few remained in use with training units and the last official USAF F-86F flight took place on June 27, 1966. The F-86H continued in service with the USAF until early 1958 and then with the Air National Guard until 1970. Surplus F-86Hs were then converted into target drones, the last of which was expended in January 1981.

Overall, a total of 9860 F-86s were built, including the F-86D, K and L. ●

NORTH AMERICAN F-86F-35-NA SABRE

North American F-86F-35-NA Sabre, 53-1192, FU-192, SkyBlazers Demonstration Team, 48th Fighter Bomber Wing, Chaumont air base, France, 1954. The SkyBlazers demonstration team used the F-86F from 1954 to 1956 before re-equipping with the F-100C aircraft which it flew until its disbandment in 1962.

NORTH AMERICAN
F-86D SABRE DOG

Almost but not quite a completely different aircraft from earlier members of the F-86 family, the single seat F-86D was designed as a radar-equipped interceptor. Less agile than the F-86A, E or F, the D it was nevertheless the USAF's first step on the road to later radar- and missile-equipped fighters.

1949-1965

N orth American's project NA-164 began on March 28, 1949, and a production version was designed as the NA-165 in April. A mock-up followed on June 1, 1949. The aircraft was equipped with a 18in diameter Westinghouse AN/APG-36 radar dish in a nose which jutted out above a truncated air intake. The fire control system was initially a Hughes E-3 and later an E-4.

A clamshell canopy was fitted to improve the pilot's chances of escape in the event of ejection but the wings,

▲ NORTH AMERICAN F-86D-35-NA SABRE

North American F-86D-35-NA Sabre, 51-8291, FU-291, 85th Fighter-Interceptor Squadron, Scott Air Force Base, Illinois, 1954. The 85th FIS used the F-86D Sabre Dog from 1954 until 1957, when it received the improved F-86L version. The squadron was part of the Air Defense Command.

NORTH AMERICAN F-86D-50-NA SABRE

North American F-86D-50-NA Sabre, 52-10006, FU-006, 4th Fighter-Interceptor Squadron, Misawa Air Base, Japan, 1956. From 1954 to 1960, equipped with F-86D, the *Fightin' Fuujins* assisted in the air defence of Japan.

NORTH AMERICAN F-86D-60-NA SABRE

North American F-86D-60-NA Sabre/53-4070 FU-070, 498th Fighter-Interceptor Squadron, Geiger Field, Washington, 1956. The Geiger Tigers operated the F-86D from 1955 to 1956, with the squadron's aircraft featuring a shark-mouth design. The unit kept the Sabre Dog until it was replaced by the F-102A Delta Dagger.

undercarriage and fin came from the F-86A. The 'all-flying' tailplane of the F-86E was fitted but without dihedral and the reshaped fuselage allowed an increase in internal fuel capacity. Armament was two dozen 2.75in unguided rockets beneath the forward fuselage.

The aircraft would be directed to its target by ground control before the pilot took over and conducted the attack using a radar screen mounted in his main instrument panel.

The first prototype made its flight debut on December 27, 1949, under the designation F-95A and shared only 25% of its components with the F-86. However, its name was changed to F-86D in July 1950 so that Congress would not find itself having to approve funds for a whole 'new' aircraft rather than a variant of an existing one.

The rocket rack was first test-fired in February 1951 and the first production F-86D flew on June 8 of that year. The 'D' had a service ceiling of 55,400ft and

therefore required a system where air from the engine was piped to the wings, fin and intake leading edges to prevent them from icing up. Air Defense Command was so impressed with the F-86D's speed and altitude performance it opted to equip two thirds of its wings with them.

The USAF received its first F-86D for testing on March 12, 1952, and the first front-line fighter squadron to receive it was the 94th Fighter-Interceptor Squadron in February 1953. Pilots took longer to train on the F-86D than on most other types since they had to be able to not only fly the aircraft and manage its weapons but also operate its radar too. A number of minor changes during the aircraft's production run necessitated 'Project Pull Out' in 1955, when 1128 F-86Ds were modified to the same standard – block F-86D-45.

Starting in May 1956, a total of 981 F-86Ds were converted into F-86Ls with the installation of Semi Automatic

NORTH AMERICAN F-86D-50-NA SABRE

North American F-86D-50-NA Sabre, 52-10030, FU-030, 512th Fighter-Interceptor Squadron, RAF Bentwaters, UK, 1956. Part of the USAFE, the main mission of the 512th FIS's Sabres was to assist in Britain's air defence. This aircraft is shown with its Mighty Mouse rocket tray extended. Sabre Dogs were not equipped with guns, relying on their air-to-air rockets instead.

Ground Environment or SAGE equipment – allowing ground control to communicate data directly to the FCS rather than having to relay it vocally to the pilot. The aircraft also received radar upgrades, extended wingtips and wing leading edges, a revised cockpit layout and an uprated engine.

A total of 2847 F-86D airframes were manufactured and the last ones – F-86Ls – left Air National Guard service during the summer of 1965.●

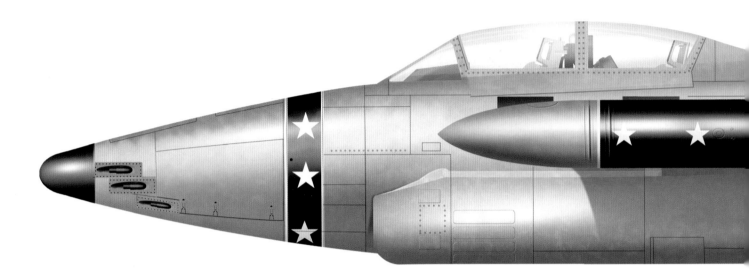

NORTHROP F-89

1948-1969

Heavily armed and sturdy but underpowered, the F-89 two-seat all-weather interceptor enjoyed a long career defending American airspace – equipping 36 active USAF units and 17 Air National Guard squadrons – though it never fired a shot in anger.

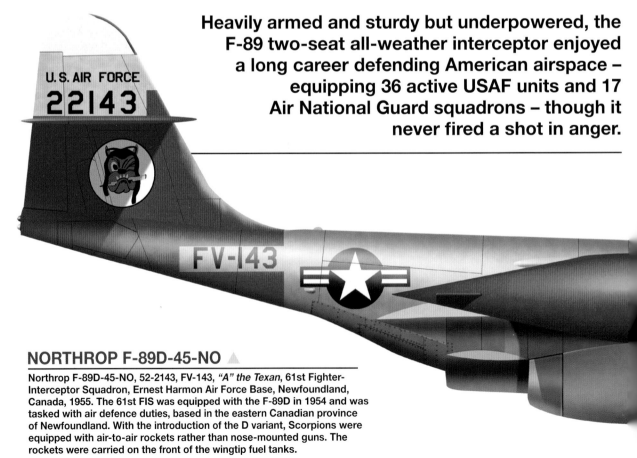

U.S. AIR FORCE
22143

FV-143

NORTHROP F-89D-45-NO ▲

Northrop F-89D-45-NO, 52-2143, FV-143, *"A" the Texan*, 61st Fighter-Interceptor Squadron, Ernest Harmon Air Force Base, Newfoundland, Canada, 1955. The 61st FIS was equipped with the F-89D in 1954 and was tasked with air defence duties, based in the eastern Canadian province of Newfoundland. With the introduction of the D variant, Scorpions were equipped with air-to-air rockets rather than nose-mounted guns. The rockets were carried on the front of the wingtip fuel tanks.

NORTHROP F-89C-25-NO

Northrop F-89C-25-NO, 51-5764, FV-764, 57th Fighter-Interceptor Squadron, Black Knights, Presque Isle Air Force Base, Maine, 1953. The Black Knights were based at Presque Island from 1953 until the following year, when the squadron was relocated to Keflavik air base, in Iceland, remaining there until 1995. The C variant was equipped with six nose-mounted 20mm guns.

U.S. AIR FORCE
15764

FV-764

SCORPION

The USAAF wanted a fast-moving replacement for the Northrop P-61 Black Widow night fighter as the war in the Pacific drew to a close and on August 28, 1945, a preliminary specification was issued.

This called for an aircraft with two engines and an armament of either six 0.6in machine guns or 20mm autocannon. Top speed had to be

530mph – which made it highly likely that the winning design would be jet-propelled. Six companies submitted proposals and the choice was soon narrowed down to two in March 1946 – what would become Curtiss-Wright's XP-87 Blackhawk and Northrop's N-24.

While the XP-87 had its engines slung beneath its wings, the N-24 had them built into the underside of its fuselage to reduce drag. The cockpit of the

former had its crew seated side-by-side, whereas the N-24 positioned them in tandem. Both were to be fitted with both nose and tail gun turrets.

Contracts were issued for the construction of prototypes for both aircraft and the N-24 was given the XP-89 designation. A mock-up of the latter was inspected and approved on June 13, 1946. The first XP-87 made its flight debut on March 1, 1948, with ▶

Northrop F-89 Scorpion

NORTHROP F-89D-45-NO SCORPION

Northrop F-89D-45-NO, 52-1959, FY-959, 59th Fighter-Interceptor Squadron, Goose Air Base, Labrador, Canada, 1955. The 59th FIS, based in Labrador Province, Canada; it was equipped with both D and J variants of the Scorpion from 1954 to 1960. The squadron was a component of the Air Defense Command (Eastern Sector).

NORTHROP F-89H-5-NO SCORPION ▷

Northrop F-89H-5-NO Scorpion 54-402 76th Fighter-Interceptor Squadron, Pinecastle Air Force Base (later McCoy Air Force Base), Florida, 1957. Operating Scorpions from 1955 to 1961, the 76th FIS was equipped with the H from 1957 to 1959.

the XF-89 followed on August 16 – the USAF having changed its designation system from 'P' to 'F' in the meantime. The latter, powered by Allison J35-A-9 turbojets, was underpowered but still managed to perform better than the lumbering Westinghouse J34-WE-7 powered Blackhawk.

As a result, the XF-87 was cancelled on October 10, 1948, and the two prototype examples were scrapped. The loss of the contract sank Curtiss-Wright as a company too, with its aviation assets being sold off to North American.

A second prototype of the XF-89 – given the name 'Scorpion' by Northrop due to its high tail – was nearly complete when the USAF decided that Northrop needed to address its poor power to weight ratio with a new powerplant:

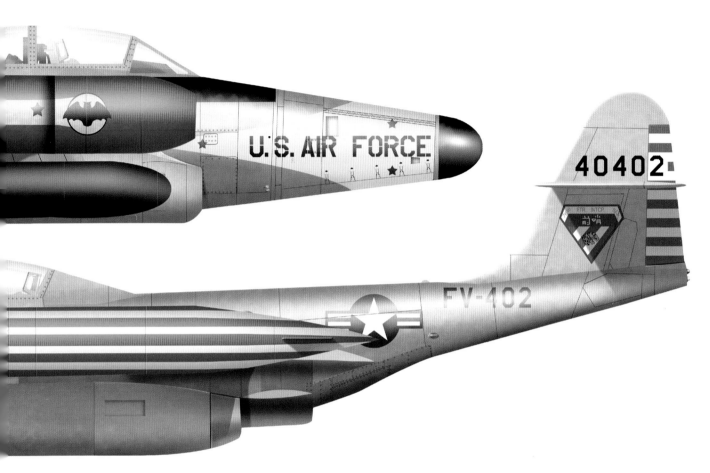

Allison's J33-A-21 with afterburner. The turret nose was deleted from the design to save weight and replaced with six fixed forward-firing guns. This necessitated a completely new nose, adding 3ft to the overall length of the aircraft. Permanent 300 gallon wingtip fuel tanks were also necessary to increase the aircraft's range as a night fighter.

While all these changes were being implemented, the USAF decided to buy Northrop some time by commissioning Lockheed to build an interim night-fighter out of the T-33 Starfire trainer – which became the F-94 Starfire and is covered elsewhere in this publication.

On May 13, 1949, the USAF awarded Northrop a contract for 48 F-89A aircraft and the first full production model flew

for the first time in September 1950. In the end, just 18 F-89As were completed before production switched to the F-89B with upgraded avionics. When this type entered service with the 84th Fighter-Interceptor Squadron in June 1951 it was soon discovered that its engine had serious problems and there were a host of other issues with on board systems. Only 40 were made.

NORTHROP F-89D-65-NO

Northrop F-89D-65-NO, 53-2639, FV-639, 321st Fighter-Interceptor Squadron, Paine Air Force Base, Washington, 1956. The F-89D equipped the 321st FIS for just a year from 1956 to 1957 before it was replaced by the H and later the J.

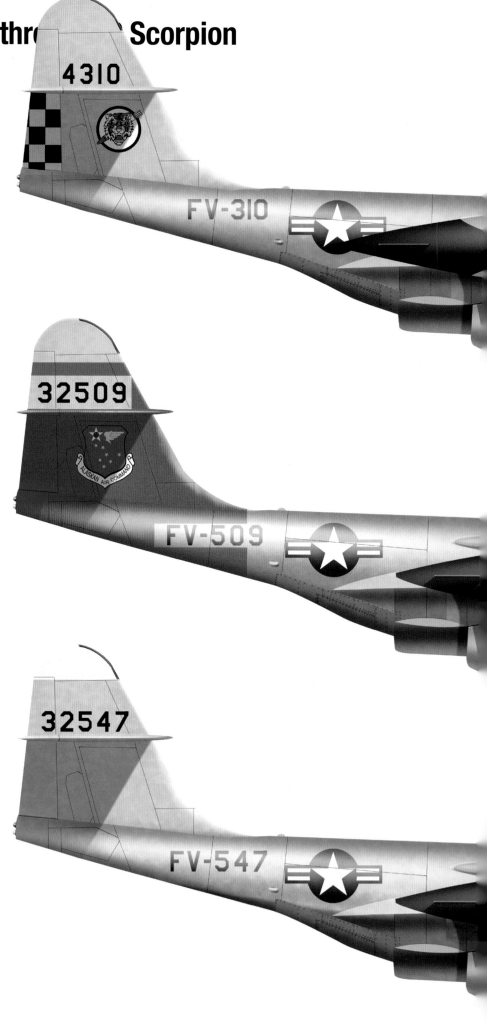

Attempts were made to cure the problems with the revised F-89C, and even though the same issues persisted a total of 164 were produced. A structural wing design weakness was then identified which affected every F-89 built to that point and all As, Bs and Cs had to be refitted with stronger wings plus new fins at the end of their wingtip tanks to reduce aerodynamic stress.

The situation was finally resolved with the F-89D, which incorporated all the fixes used up to that point and finally deleted the cannon nose, replacing it with the Hughes E-6 fire control system and wingtip pods housing a total of fifty-two 2.75in FFAR rockets. Two different proposals to re-engine the Scorpion as the F-89E (with Allison J71 turbojets) and F (with General Electric J47s) were put forward and dismissed, as were plans for an F-89G which would have carried AIM-4 Falcon missiles linked to a Hughes MA-1 fire control – giving it a similar offensive capability to the F-106 Delta Dart detailed elsewhere in this publication.

Instead, however, the F-89H was produced. It incorporated a Hughes E-9 fire control system linked to three Falcons in each wingtip pod and an option to fit another three under each wing on pylons. This provided a significant offensive capability but the extra weight also served to significantly degrade the Scorpion's performance. Just 156 were made and despite having only entered service in March 1956, all examples had been transferred to the Air National Guard by September 1959.

Incredibly, despite newer fighters with much better performance starting to become available, Northrop was still able to get another variant of the F-89 approved for development – the F-89J. No new examples were built but a total of 350 F-86Ds were upgraded to J standard. As the F-89J, they carried wingtip fuel tanks rather than rockets and their weaponry was limited to a single Douglas MB-1 (later AIR-2) Genie unguided nuclear-tipped rocket slung beneath each wing. An F-89J carried out the only live test of a Genie during Operation Plumbob over the Nevada Test Site on July 19, 1957.

Overall, 1050 F-89s were manufactured and while the USAF's Air Defense Command retired its remaining examples during 1962, the Scorpion continued to serve with the Air National Guard up to July 1969 before finally being phased out.

Given the slow pace of its development, its lacklustre performance and its various technical problems, it is remarkable that the Scorpion continued to serve as long as it did. It quickly became obsolete – being surpassed in performance by much more capable aircraft.●

NORTHROP F-89H-1-NO 54-310

Northrop F-89H-1-NO 54-310, FV-310, 437th Fighter-Interceptor Squadron, Oxnard Air Force Base, California, 1956. Several versions of the Scorpion were flown by the 437th FIS from 1955 to 1960. The H variant introduced a new wingtip tank capable of internally carrying three AIM-4 Falcon air-to-air missiles. In the image, the missiles are ready to be fired.

NORTHROP F-89J-55-NO SCORPION 53-2509

Northrop F-89J-55-NO Scorpion 53-2509, 449th Fighter Interceptor Squadron, Ladd AFB, Alaska, 1958. The 449th FIS was assigned to the 11th Air Division (Defense) and tasked with air defense for the Northern part of Alaska. The F-89J could carry a single AIR-2 Genie nuclear-tipped rocket and two AIM-4 Falcons in each wing; it was also capable of carrying air-to-air rockets in its wingtip tanks.

NORTHROP F-89J SCORPION, OPERATION PLUMBOB

Operation Plumbob was carried out between May 28 and October 7, 1958, and encompassed a total of 29 nuclear test explosions. One of the weapons tested, the 'John' shot, was an AIR-2 Genie air-to-air rocket fired from an F-89J Scorpion – the only time a Genie with a live nuclear warhead was ever launched. The test was highly publicised, with five officers and a photographer filmed standing at ground zero directly beneath the blast when it went off on July 19 at 2pm.

LOCKHEED F-94B-5-LO STARFIRE

Lockheed F-94B-5-LO 51-5449, FA-449, 319th Fighter-Interceptor Squadron, Suwon Air Base (K-13), South Korea,1953. The 319th FIS was one of several all-weather interceptor squadrons deployed to Korea. FV-449 made the squadron's first Korean air-to-air kill, shooting down a "propeller aircraft" (possible a Lavochkin LA-9-R), on January 30, 1953.

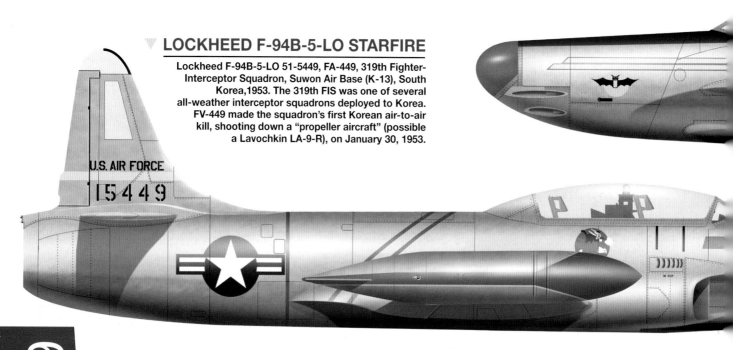

1949-1959

LOCKHEED F-94 STARFIRE

The F-94 all-weather interceptor was rapidly developed from Lockheed's two-seater trainer Shooting Star variant, the T-33, and could therefore be regarded as the ultimate development of the F-80. While it was never outstanding, it still enjoyed a long career for a type intended as a stopgap.

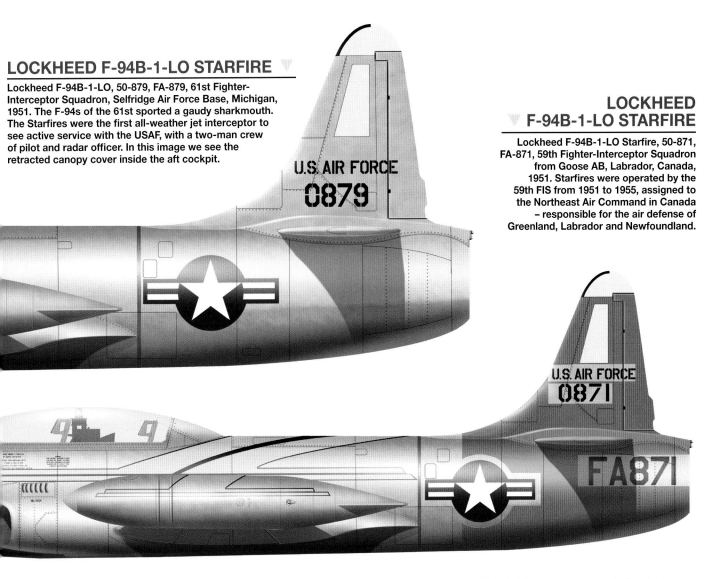

LOCKHEED F-94B-1-LO STARFIRE ▽

Lockheed F-94B-1-LO, 50-879, FA-879, 61st Fighter-Interceptor Squadron, Selfridge Air Force Base, Michigan, 1951. The F-94s of the 61st sported a gaudy sharkmouth. The Starfires were the first all-weather jet interceptor to see active service with the USAF, with a two-man crew of pilot and radar officer. In this image we see the retracted canopy cover inside the aft cockpit.

LOCKHEED F-94B-1-LO STARFIRE ▽

Lockheed F-94B-1-LO Starfire, 50-871, FA-871, 59th Fighter-Interceptor Squadron from Goose AB, Labrador, Canada, 1951. Starfires were operated by the 59th FIS from 1951 to 1955, assigned to the Northeast Air Command in Canada – responsible for the air defense of Greenland, Labrador and Newfoundland.

Getting the USAF's chosen all-weather and night fighter, the Northrop F-89, up to scratch in 1948 was obviously going to take time and it was clear that there was a gap in American capabilities which needed to be filled.

In December 1948, the air force therefore turned to Lockheed – now famous for turning the P-80 around in record time – and asked whether it could design and build a new two-seater equipped with the Hughes E-1 radar within a year. Lockheed looked carefully at the job and decided that it was achievable.

Kelly Johnson and his team took the existing two-seat version of the proven F-80, the T-33, and rebuilt it to meet the USAF's requirements. The airframe was fitted with six 0.5in cannon, a completely new nose and a new engine – the T-33's J33 engine was replaced with an Allison J33-A-33 – which came with one of the world's first production afterburners.

When it became clear that Lockheed's new fighter was rapidly coming together, the USAF placed an order for 110 examples and gave it the designation

F-94A. The prototype made its flight debut on April 16, 1949, having taken just 13 weeks to complete.

Early flight tests found centre of gravity issues with the six guns, corrected when two of them were removed, and the T-33's wingtip fuel tanks – which extended from the tips – were replaced with tanks slung beneath the tips instead.

With these alterations made, the first production F-94As were ready for delivery to the USAF for testing and acceptance in December 1949 – just a year after the USAF asked Lockheed whether the aircraft was even feasible. The first unit to receive it was the 325th All-Weather Fighter Squadron in June 1950, just in time for the beginning of the Korean War.

The F-94 replaced the piston-engined F-82Fs of the 317th, 318th and 319th squadrons as an interceptor – ready to ▶

LOCKHEED F-94B-5-LO STARFIRE ▽

Lockheed F-94B-5-LO Starfire, 51-5480, FA-480, 68th Fighter-Interceptor Squadron, Itazuke Air Base, Japan, 1954. Based in Japan, detachments of the 68th FIS were deployed to several air bases in Korea during the conflict.

Lockheed F-94 Starfire

LOCKHEED F-94C-1-LO STARFIRE ▽

Lockheed F-94C-1-LO Starfire, 51-13547, FA-547, 29th Fighter-Interceptor Squadron, Great
Falls Air Force Base (later Malmstrom AFB), Montana, 1954. The 29th FIS was equipped
with the C variant of the Starfire from 1953 to 1957, assigned to the 29th Air Division.
This was part of Air Defense Command and responsible for protecting Montana,
Idaho, Wyoming, North Dakota, South Dakota and Nebraska
and parts of Nevada, Utah, and Colorado.

tackle any Soviet bombers that might
attack.

During combat operations in Korea
it became clear that the F-94A's
endurance was severely limited by
its thirsty afterburner and the weight
of its radar equipment. As a result,
Lockheed modified the design to create
the F-94B. This included larger more
capacious tip tanks, strengthened
landing gear, improved hydraulics,
a new autopilot and improved flight
instruments. The USAF ordered a total
of 357 F-94Bs.

But as early as 1949, Lockheed
had laid plans for an even better all-
weather and night fighter. The F-94
was to be given new thinner wings,
swept tailplanes, a braking parachute,
a new Westinghouse autopilot and
another new engine – the Pratt &
Whitney J48-P-5, based on the British

Rolls-Royce RB.44 Tay turbojet (itself an
enlarged version of the Rolls-Royce Nene).

A Hughes fire control system was to be
installed, linked to the autopilot, and 24
forward firing aircraft rockets (FFARs) in
four groups of six were positioned around
the aircraft's nose.

Even with the F-89 entering service,
in late 1950 the USAF decided to order
Lockheed's new F-94 under a new
designation – the F-97A. Again, an order
was placed for 110 aircraft but under the
designation F-94C, although the type was
given the new name Starfire.

Deliveries of the new F-94C began in
July 1951 and in 1953 an extra 12-rocket
pod was added to each wing. By May
1954 a total of 387 had been delivered
thanks to a series of additional orders.

The older F-94As and Bs were phased
out during early 1954 and replaced by
F-89Cs and Ds along with F-86Ds. They

would continue to serve with the Air
National Guard, however. The F-94C was
retired from active service with the USAF
in November 1957 and by the Air National
Guard during the summer of 1959.

The F-94 proved to be a fitting last
hurrah for the P-80/F-80 Shooting Star.
Despite being rushed into service, it
proved reliable and rugged – precisely
what the USAF needed and delivered
exactly when it needed it.●

THE OLDER F-94As AND Bs WERE PHASED OUT DURING EARLY 1954 AND REPLACED BY F-89Cs AND Ds ALONG WITH F-86Ds.

LOCKHEED F-94C-1-LO STARFIRE

Lockheed F-94C-1-LO Starfire, 50-1063, FA-063, 354th Fighter-Interceptor Squadron, Oxnard Air Force Base, California, 1954. Integrated into the 533rd Air Defense Group/27th Air Division, the 354th FIS was equipped with F-94Cs from 1953 to 1955. It was assigned to defend Southern California.

LOCKHEED F-94C-1-LO STARFIRE

Lockheed F-94C-1-LO Starfire 51-13555, FA-555, 27th Fighter-Interceptor Squadron, Griffiss Air Force Base, New York, 1955. The 27th Fighter-Interceptor Squadron converted form the B variant of the Starfire to the C in 1954, operating it until 1956, when the squadron was disbanded.

LOCKHEED F-94C-1-LO STARFIRE

Lockheed F-94C-1-LO Starfire 51-13600, FA-600, 46th Fighter-Interceptor Squadron, Dover Air Force Base, Delaware, 1953-1958. Operating the F-94C for five years, the 46th FIS was assigned to the 4710th Air Defense Wing, responsible for the air defense of southeastern Pennsylvania, south New Jersey, Delaware and Maryland.

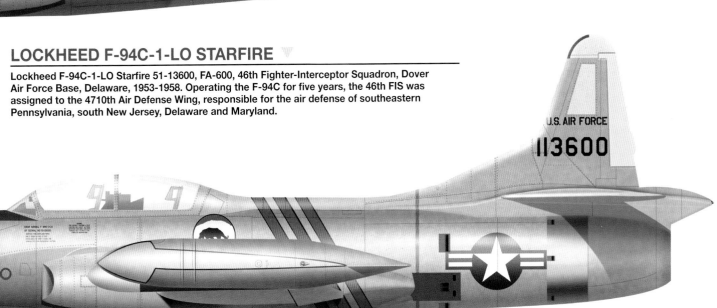

41821

FW

NORTH AMERICAN F-100 SUPER SABRE

North American's rugged Super Sabre was the first operational USAF aircraft capable of going supersonic in level flight and the first of the 'Century Series'. It was designed to replace the company's original Sabre as a fighter – hence the name – but excelled as a fighter-bomber instead.

NORTH-AMERICAN F-100C-15-NA SUPER SABRE

North-American F-100C-15-NA Super Sabre, 54-1821, FW-821, 450th Fighter Day Wing, Foster AFB, Texas, 1955. With the Introduction of the F-100C, the USAF was provided with a fighter-bomber version of the Super Sabre. The variant entered USAF service in 1955 with the 450th FDW.

W ork on creating a Sabre capable of breaking the sound barrier commenced in February 1949 with a series of in-house studies at North American by the company's Raymond Rice and Edgar Schmuel. It was hoped that increasing the sweepback angle of the F-86's wings from 35 to 45 , adopting area rule for the fuselage and fitting a more powerful turbojet would be enough.

A proposal for an 'Advanced F-86D' which incorporated these design elements was submitted to the USAF but rejected. North American tried again with an 'Advanced F-86E', which featured a more slender fuselage and a

redesigned nose intake but despite these improvements the design could not offer a radical leap forward in performance – in an age when other manufacturers were promising Mach 2 and beyond.

A third proposal, the NA-180 Sabre 45, rolled all the novel features of its two predecessors into a single package. Very little of the original aircraft now remained – the Sabre 45 being substantially bigger and heavier. Fitted with the Pratt & Whitney J57-P-1 afterburning turbojet it was also significantly faster and more powerful.

North American had intended to equip the Sabre 45 with radar to make it a useful interceptor capable of replacing the F-86D but again the USAF wasn't

interested. What the air force really wanted was a straightforward high-performance cannon-armed day fighter and it caused North American little difficulty to design out the radar and include a bigger nose intake instead. The Sabre 45 was to be armed with a quartet of 20mm cannon.

It was now 1951 and the F-86 Sabre was gaining the upper hand over the MiG-15 but the air force was well aware that this advantage was largely due to ▶

NORTH-AMERICAN F-100A-10-NA SUPER SABRE

North-American F-100A-10-NA Super Sabre, 53-1700, FW-700, 434th Fighter Day Squadron, 479th Fighter Day Wing, George AFB, California, 1955. The F-100A officially entered USAF service on September 1954, with the 479th Fighter Wing at George AFB, California. This is a later A variant featuring the enlarged fin.

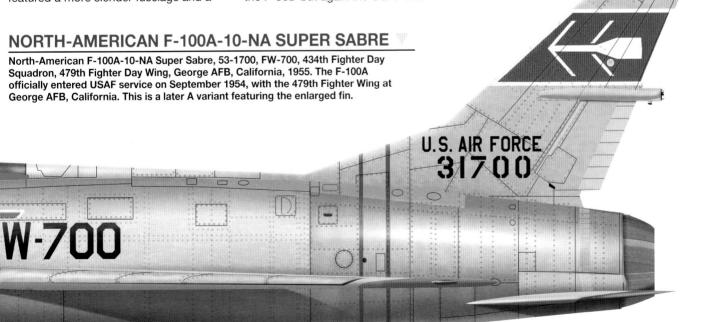

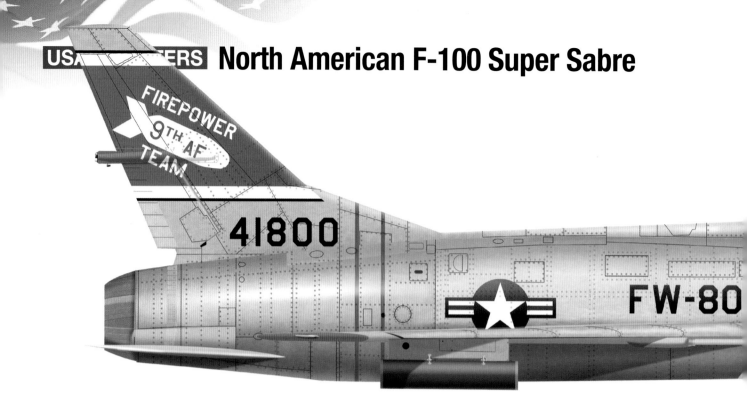

North American F-100 Super Sabre

the superior training and experience of its pilots rather than the F-86's own innate qualities. A Sabre replacement was urgently needed that would give the USAF a significant technical advantage over the communists' Soviet-designed equipment.

Despite some concerns that the Sabre 45 would be too complicated and expensive for a mass-produced day fighter, the USAF Council decided to press ahead with the type in October 1951. At the beginning of November the air force gave North American a Letter Contract for a pair of Sabre 45 (NA-180) prototypes and 110 NA-192 full production models. The USAF's

eagerness to bring the type into service was plain and based on this plan North American would be building the prototypes on production jigs and racking up components for the production series even before the first aircraft had flown.

A mock-up inspection took place on November 9, resulting in requests for more than 100 separate changes to the design. The cockpit canopy was extended, the tailplanes were moved lower down and the shape of the fuselage was altered.

The new type was given the F-100 designation in December 1951. More than six months later a further series of

last minute changes were made – the self-sealing fuel tanks were to be swapped for lighter non-self-sealing tanks, the aircraft's nose was lengthened by 9in, the tailplanes and fin were made slightly shorter with increased chord and fixings for external weapons racks were added.

In October 1952, the USAF asked North American to see whether wing fuel tanks could be designed for the F-100 to increase its radius of action and development work on this began.

North American's Los Angeles workshops completed the first YF-100A prototype, serial 52-5754, on April 24, 1953. It was powered by a pair of Pratt

NORTH-AMERICAN
F-100C-25-NA SUPER SABRE ▷

North-American F-100C-25-NA Super Sabre, 54-1984, FW-984, 53rd Fighter Day Squadron, 36th Fighter Day Wing, Landstuhl Air Base (later Ramstein Air Base), West Germany, 1956.

NORTH-AMERICAN
F-100D-25-NA SUPER SABRE ▷

North-American F-100D-25-NA Super Sabre, 55-3637, FW-637, 79th Tactical Fighter Squadron, 20th Tactical Fighter Wing, RAF Woodbridge, UK, 1960. The 79th TFS was tasked with supporting NATO forces both in conventional and nuclear roles.

◄ NORTH-AMERICAN F-100C-5-NA SUPER SABRE

North-American F-100C-5-NA Super Sabre, 54-1800, FW-800, 333rd Tactical Fighter Squadron, 4th Tactical Fighter Wing, Seymour Johnson Air Force Base, North Carolina, 1958. This aircraft wore a special paint job during TAC's Tactical Fighter Weapons Meet of 1958; the squadron representing the Ninth Air Force in the competition held at Nellis AFB.

& Whitney J57-P-7 engines normally capable of 9220lb thrust or 14,800 with afterburner but de-rated for test purposes. The aircraft was then moved to Edwards Air Force Base in readiness for flight testing.

With George S 'Wheaties' Welch, Second World War ace turned company test pilot, at the controls the aircraft broke the sound barrier above 30,000ft in level flight during its 55-minute maiden flight on May 25. This feat was repeated during a second flight of 20 minutes later on that same day.

Above 30,000ft the YF-100A could go supersonic with ease and could

fly close to Mach 1 even at low level. Less than two months later, on July 6, 1953, the aircraft hit Mach 1.44 while diving from an altitude of 51,000ft. That same month, the USAF followed up on its request for wing fuel tanks with a request that these same new wings should be able to carry a bomb payload.

Welch took the second prototype, 52-5755, up for its first flight on

October 14, 1953, and a press conference was held on October 19, 1953, to showcase the aircraft – the first time the public had been made aware of the F-100 programme's existence. Welch shocked the assembled journalists by ▶

USAF FIGHTERS North American F-100 Super Sabre

NORTH AMERICAN F-100D-50-NH SUPER SABRE

North American F-100D-50-NH Super Sabre, 55-2907, FW-907, 614th Tactical Fighter Squadron, England Air Force Base, Louisiana, 1961. Stationed at England AFB, Louisiana, the 614th TFS was deployed to several locations in Europe and the Middle East in support of NATO, before being deployed to Vietnam.

NORTH-AMERICAN F-100D-25-NA

North-American F-100D-25-NA, 55-3604, 416th Tactical Fighter Squadron, 3rd Tactical Fighter Wing, Bien Hoa AB, South Vietnam, 1966. F-100s or 'Huns' were deployed to Vietnam early on in the conflict, with the first aircraft arriving in 1961. The 416th TFS was moved to Vietnam air bases in 1965. This aircraft has a 0 prefix to its military registration signifying that is an aircraft with over 10 years' service.

NORTH-AMERICAN F-100D-90-NA

North-American F-100D-90-NA, 56-3264, FW-264, 510th Tactical Fighter Squadron, Langley AFB, Virginia, Bien Hoa AB, South Vietnam, 1967. The 510th TFS was deployed to Vietnam from 1964 to 1969, the year when it was deactivated. It would be reactivated 25 years later in 1994.

shooting past the press grandstand at around Mach 1 just feet from the ground and succeeded in shattering the windows of the Palmdale airport administration building with the resulting sonic boom.

Only a week later the first production model F-100A – serial 52-5756 – took to the air. Second World War veteran Colonel Frank Kendall 'Pete' Everest set a new world air speed record of 755.149mph in the aircraft on the same day. This broke the existing 752.9mph

record set only 26 days earlier by James B Verdin of the US Navy flying a Douglas F4D Skyray.

Naturally, North American's public relations department had a field day – declaring that the company had built the world's first operational supersonic fighter. Unfortunately this proved to be somewhat premature, since the type was not yet actually in operational service and testing had only just begun.

Although he was impressed by its unprecedented straight line performance,

Everest found that poor visibility from the cockpit made take-offs and landings tricky and the sharply swept wings meant landing speed was necessarily high – which only compounded the problem. Similarly, the type proved to be a handful when flying at low speed and longitudinal stability was lacking at high speed.

Early flights showed that some rudder flutter was present too, but this was corrected using hydraulic dampers. Nevertheless, test pilots agreed that taken together these various issues and ▶

NORTH AMERICAN F-100D-20-NA SUPER SABRE

North American F-100D-20-NA Super Sabre, 55-3568, FW-568, 35th Tactical Fighter Squadron, 8th Fighter Bomber Wing, Itazuke AB, Japan, 1959. Super Sabres also had a tactical nuclear bombing capability; this 35th FBS aircraft is depicted carrying a Mark 7 bomb.

an overall lack of flight testing meant the aircraft was not yet fit for front line service – but their reports were set aside and preparations to get the type delivered to USAF squadrons continued unabated.

The 479th Fighter Day Wing of Tactical Air Command, based at George Air Force Base, began to receive its first F-100As at the end of November 1953 and a month later the USAF decided that the last 70 F-100As should be modified to become NA-214 fighter-bombers with the new fuel and bomb load-carrying wing – later to be redesignated F-100Cs. The USAF then placed an order for another 230 F-100Cs on February 24, 1954. By May 27 the total number of F-100Cs on order had increased to 564.

The fourth production model F-100A became the YF-100C prototype and although its wings could not be retrofitted with internal fuel tanks they were adapted to accept drop tanks or up to 5000lb of stores. The tips were extended by 12in too – a modification later carried over onto the F-100A production line – and the F-100C benefitted from an in-flight refuelling probe fitted beneath the starboard wing.

On September 27, 1954, and order was made to complete many of the pre-ordered F-100Cs as F-100Ds instead and two days later the first F-100A unit, the 479th Fighter Day Wing, finally became operational.

NORTH-AMERICAN F-100D-90-NA SUPER SABRE ▽

North-American F-100D-90-NA Super Sabre, 56-3339, 90th Tactical Fighter Squadron, 3rd Tactical Fighter Wing, Bien Hoa AB, South Vietnam, 1966.

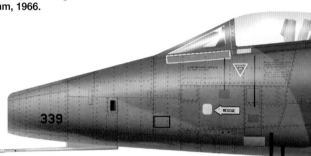

The F-100D would incorporate a wide range of alterations to the basic F-100 design and would correct many of the issues raised during the aircraft's hurried development and introduction. Once again, a new wing was fitted – this time with a greater chord at the wingroot due to less swept inner flaps which increased surface area and lowered landing speed. The underwing pylons could be jettisoned using explosive bolts rather than relying on gravity and a new centreline hardpoint was introduced. The F-100D also featured built-in electronic countermeasures equipment, the AN/

AJB-1 low-altitude bombing system and an AN/APS-54 tail warning radar.

But even as plans were being laid for this much improved design, the F-100A still harboured a significant flaw which was yet to really make itself felt: the aircraft's fin was too small and too weak, which meant the aircraft suffered from directional instability and the fin itself was put under a dangerous degree of strain during extreme manoeuvring. Fitting drop tanks made this even worse.

Welch was killed on October 12, 1954, when the F-100A he was flying – the ninth production model, 52-5764 – broke

THE F-100A STILL HARBOURED A SIGNIFICANT FLAW WHICH WAS YET TO REALLY MAKE ITSELF FELT: THE AIRCRAFT'S FIN WAS TOO SMALL AND TOO WEAK.

USAF
0-63339

up during a test dive and recovery. Another experienced pilot, Geoffrey Stephenson of the RAF's Central Fighter Establishment, who had been evaluating the F-100A, died in similar circumstances soon after. And a third pilot, Major Frank N Emory, narrowly escape with his life when his F-100A also disintegrated during high-g manoeuvring.

All 180 remaining F-100As were grounded – 68 of them already in service and 112 ready to be delivered – and North American quickly set about investigating the problem and working up a solution. It soon became apparently

that changes to the fin were necessary and a lengthened version with 27% more vertical area was designed.

In the meantime, the first production F-100C was completed on October 19 and conditionally accepted ten days later despite the flight ban still in force.

The newly enlarged fin was introduced to the Los Angeles assembly line in early 1955 and the 184th F-100A was built with it. The remaining F-100As were soon brought up to the same standard and the grounding order was lifted on the upgraded aircraft. As a result, the first F-100C was able to make its first ▶

52894

◢ NORTH-AMERICAN F-100D-50-NH SUPER SABRE

North-American F-100D-50-NH Super Sabre, 55-2894, 416th Tactical Fighter Squadron, 3rd Tactical Fighter Wing, Bien Hoa AB, South Vietnam, 1965. During a mission escorting F-105s on April 4, 1965, F-100s got involved in the first USAF air-to-air combat involving jets in the Vietnam War. One of the planes was flown by Captain Donald W. Kilgus, who scored a kill against a MiG-17.

◀ NORTH-AMERICAN F-100D-20-NA SUPER SABRE

North-American F-100D-20-NA Super Sabre, 55-3550, 308th Tactical Fighter Squadron, 31st Tactical Fighter Wing, Phan Rang AB, South Vietnam, September 1970. This aircraft would be the last F-100 shot down during the conflict.

North American F-100 Super Sabre

NORTH-AMERICAN F-100D-20-NA SUPER SABRE ▽

North-American F-100D-20-NA Super Sabre, 55-3520, Six, 4520th Air Demonstration Squadron, Thunderbirds, Nellis Air force Base, Nevada, 1961. The famous aerobatic team used Super Sabres from 1956 to 1966; in 1964 the team converted to the Republic F-105, but following an accident reverted back to the Hun.

NORTH-AMERICAN F-100F-10-NA SUPER SABRE ▽

North-American F-100F-10-NA Super Sabre, 56-3837, 416th Tactical Fighter Squadron, 37th Tactical Fighter Wing, Phu Cat Air Base, South Vietnam, 1968. In Vietnam, F-100Fs from the 37th TFW, were used as 'Misty' forward air controllers (FACs), flying at low altitude to track and mark enemy targets for subsequent attacks.

NORTH-AMERICAN F-100F-10-NA SUPER SABRE ▷

North-American F-100F-10-NA Super Sabre, 56-3836, 615th Tactical Fighter Squadron, 35th Tactical Fighter Wing, Phan Rang Air Base, South Vietnam, 1967. F-100s were used in MiGCAP missions in Vietnam. Both single and two-seat variants were equipped with air-to-air missiles to perform these operations. In this image an F-100F is shown equipped with a double AIM-9B sidewinder launcher.

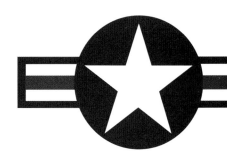

flight on January 17, 1955, and deliveries of the type to the 450th Fighter Day Squadron began in April.

Delivery of the last F-100As was completed that July – the same month that the 450th became operational – and on August 20, 1955, Colonel Harold Hanes set the second F-100 air-speed world record in a row – taking the first F-100C up to 822.135mph. North American received a contract to build a two-seat trainer F-100, the TF-100C, in December 1955.

The first F-100D took to the air on January 24, 1956, and beginning on May 19, 1956, the USAF's Thunderbirds display team were re-equipped with F-100Cs. The first and only TF-100C made its flight debut on August 3, 1956, but was later destroyed following a spinning test from which it failed to recover.

The first deliveries of the F-100D were made to the 405th Fighter-Bomber Wing at Langley Air Force Base in September 1956.

Early problems with the F-100D, including unreliable electrics, engine problems, malfunctioning bomb release systems and an inaccurate fire control system were gradually overcome through various updates and upgrades while the aircraft was in service. Following on from the tests carried out with the TF-100C, a full production two-seater, the F-100F, made its first flight on March 7, 1957, with deliveries commencing in January 1958.

The last F-100 rolled off the production line in October 1959 for a grand total of 2294 built. The aircraft served extensively with the USAF in Vietnam – primarily in the ground-attack role – and served abroad with Taiwan, France and Turkey. The last operational F-100 mission was flown by the Air National Guard on November 10, 1979.●

NORTH-AMERICAN F-100F-20-NA SUPER SABRE

North-American F-100F-20-NA Super Sabre, 58-1221, Wild Weasel Detachment- 6234th Tactical Fighter Wing, 388th Tactical Fighter Wing, Korat RTAFB, Thailand, 1966. With the need to counter the growing surface-to-air missile threat, specialised aircraft, crews and aircraft had to became operational in the Vietnam theatre. The first crews were deployed in 1965 with F-100Fs modified for this mission – detecting air defence radar systems so follow-up attacks could be made by other aircraft.

McDONNELL F-101 VOODOO

Measuring 67ft 5in from end to end, compared to the F-100's 50ft, the F-101 was huge, powerful and difficult to fly. Designed as a fighter, most of its service career was actually spent performing reconnaissance, nuclear bomber and interceptor duties.

32426

FIRE WALL

McDONNELL F-101A-5-MC VOODOO

McDonnell F-101A-5-MC Voodoo, 53-2426, Operation Firewall, 1957.
This aircraft set a world speed record of 1207.6mph on a ten-mile course at Edwards AFB during Operation Firewall on December 12, 1957.

U.S. AIR FORCE

60068

1954-1982

FB-068

he US Army Air Forces issued a requirement in early 1946 for a long-range 'penetration' jet fighter that could escort nuclear bombers to their targets and back. McDonnell Aircraft created the Model 36 to meet the requirement in April 1946 and the USAAF gave the company a contract to develop it as the XP-88, including an order for two prototypes, on June 20.

The design featured 35 swept wings and a radical V-tail arrangement but the latter was soon dropped in favour of a more conventional tail layout. On July 1, 1948, the two prototypes were redesignated XF-88 and XF-88A thanks to the switch from 'P' to 'F' brought about by the creation of the US Air Force as an independent service. Early on, the 'Voodoo' name was also given to the F-88 series by McDonnell.

The XF-88, powered by a pair of Westinghouse XJ34-WE-13 turbojets built into its fuselage, was completed on August 11, 1948, and first flew on October 20. Further flight testing took place in March 1949 and it was found that the aircraft lacked high-speed performance.

As a result, the XF-88A was completed with afterburners and made its maiden flight on April 26, 1949. It performed well and defeated its rivals in the 'penetration' fighter competition – Lockheed's XF-90 and North American's XF-93A – but a reduction in funding for the programme meant that the fledgling F-88 was shelved before a production contract could be issued.

Combat experience during the Korean War, however, indicated that there remained a need for a long-range bomber escort and in 1951 the USAF issued a new requirement. Although several companies submitted bids, the McDonnell F-88 was already well developed and succeeded in winning the competition.

The USAF gave McDonnell a contract to develop a reconnaissance version of the F-101 on October 11, 1953, and a mock-up inspection of the YRF-101A was made on January 13, 1954.

The first single seat F-101A, when it appeared, was largely based on the earlier design but with a number of significant improvements – the engines were massively upgraded from the 3000lb thrust J34s to Pratt & Whitney J57-P-13s with 10,200lb thrust each (15,000 with afterburners); the type's air intakes were enlarged; the tail planes were repositioned higher up the fin and the wings were increased in chord. Armament was four 20mm M39 cannon with a K-19 gunsight.

The aircraft's maiden flight was on September 29, 1954, and McDonnell test pilot Robert C Little was able to go supersonic effortlessly – the first time any new aircraft had ever broken the speed of sound on its first flight. An F-100 was being flown as a chase plane but was unable to keep up even with its own afterburners on. ▶

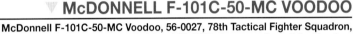

McDONNELL F-101C-50-MC VOODOO

McDonnell F-101C-50-MC Voodoo, 56-0027, 78th Tactical Fighter Squadron, 81st Tactical Fighter Wing, RAF Woodbridge, UK, 1959. A new variant of the Voodoo, the F-101C entered service with the Tactical Air Command in 1957. The aircraft were transferred to USAFE units in 1958, operating from RAF air bases.

McDONNELL RF-101C-65-MC VOODOO

McDonnell RF-101C-65-MC Voodoo, 56-0068, 20th Tactical Reconnaissance Squadron, 363rd Tactical Reconnaissance Wing, Shaw AFB, South-Carolina, 1962. During the Cuban Missile Crisis, the 363rd TRW deployed RF-101Cs, to MacDill Air Force Base, Florida. In the autumn of 1962, an intensive campaign of low-level reconnaissance flights was undertaken over Cuban territory, collecting evidence of the Soviet military buildup, including the detection of SA-2 surface-to-air missiles.

McDONNELL RF-101C-40-MC VOODOO

McDonnell RF-101C-40-MC Voodoo, 56-0166, 363rd Tactical Reconnaissance Wing, Shaw AFB, South-Carolina, 1957. During Operation Sun Run, pilots from the 363rd TRW established a set of three continental speed records. 56-0166 was one of the aircraft used during that mission on November 27, 1957.

An early problem with the F-101A was its inability to handle loads above 6.33 g. The USAF had specified 7.33 g but decided that it would take the early 6.33 g airframes as the F-101A until the type's structure could be strengthened, the modified type then being designated the F-101C.

Worse than this, though, was the aircraft's disturbing tendency to pitch up at the slightest provocation – an issue which was never adequately resolved. There were also difficulties with the

type's forwards-retracting nosewheel, which would not powerful enough to retract if the airspeed rose above 90mph.

The first test flight of the reconnaissance prototype YRF-101A was on June 30, 1955, and by now McDonnell was also busy with the F-101B – the two-seat long-range interceptor version of the aircraft. Deliveries of the F-101A to the 27th Strategic Fighter Wing finally began in May 1957, as did deliveries of the RF-101A to the 17th Tactical Reconnaissance Squadron of the 363rd

Tactical Reconnaissance Wing – the RF-101A replacing that unit's RB-57A/B Canberras.

Just two months later the 27th Strategic Fighter Wing was transferred to Tactical Air Command and became the 27th Fighter-Bomber Wing (27th FBW). The F-101A, after just two months in service as a 'fighter', was now being re-equipped as a nuclear bomber. July 1957 also saw the first flight of the RF-101C – the reconnaissance version of the new F-101C.

McDONNELL RF-101C-75-MC VOODOO

McDonnell RF-101C-75-MC Voodoo, 56-0119, 45thTactical Reconnaissance Squadron, Tan Son Nhut Air Base, South Vietnam, 1969. The RF-101C was the only variant of the Voodoo to be used in war by the USAF. The 45th TRS began operations over Vietnam early in the war and from 1962 to 1970 several detachments and squadron deployments were made to the combat area.

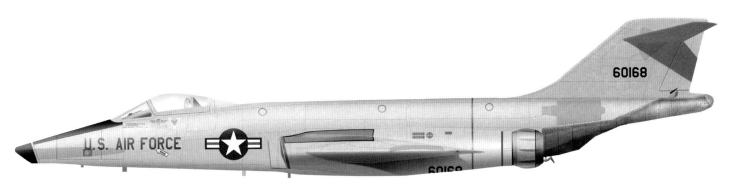

McDONNELL RF-101C-40-MC VOODOO

McDonnell RF-101C-40-MC Voodoo, 56-0168, 45th Tactical Reconnaissance Squadron, Misawa Air Base, Japan, 1958. The RF-101Cs operating in the PACAF area were painted in an overall light grey colour scheme. This was later replaced by the SEA colour scheme when the aircraft were deployed to the Vietnam conflict.

Meanwhile, less than a year after Horace Hanes had set a new air speed record in the F-100C, the record had been snatched away from the US by the British Fairey Delta 2, flown by Peter Twiss. Now the Americans had an aircraft with the straight line speed to do something about it. Major Adrian Drew of the 27th FBW flew an F-101A modified with even more powerful J57-P-53 engines to a record-breaking 1207.6mph on December 12, 1957.

The structurally strengthened F-101C

– which was otherwise almost identical to the F-101A – entered service in 1958 with the 27th FBW, which underwent another redesignation on July 7, 1958, to become the 27th Tactical Fighter Wing. The RF-101C had entered service in June 1958.

A little over a year later, on January 5, 1959, the F-101B entered service with the 60th Fighter-Interceptor Squadron. The 'B' was fitted with J57-P-55 engines and had longer afterburner units than the 'A'. It also had the Hughes MG-13 fire-control system, designed to launch nuclear ▶

McDONNELL F-101B-95-MC VOODOO

McDonnell F-101B-95-MC Voodoo, 57-0364, 60th Fighter Interceptor Squadron, Otis Air Force Base, Massachusetts, 1970. F-101Bs entered USAF service on January 5, 1959, with the 60th Fighter Interceptor Squadron. The F-101B could be armed with the nuclear AIR-2 Genie rocket.

McDonnell F-101 Voodoo

and non-nuclear air-to-air missiles and rockets including the AIM-4 Falcon and later the nuclear AIR-2 Genie.

A trainer version of the F-101 was created in 1961 under the designation F-101F. This was similar to the two-seat F-101B but had dual controls fitted. And in April of that year 56 F-101Bs and 10 F-101Fs were supplied to Canada with the aircraft receiving the designation CF-101B.

During 1964, a total of 29 old F-101As and 32 F-101Cs were converted into reconnaissance airframes as the RF-101G and RF-101H respectively. Finally, the Canadians traded 56 CF-101Bs back to the USAF in exchange for 66 'new' airframes between 1970 and 1972. These had actually been manufactured earlier that the Canadians' first batch but had lower hours on them. The Canadians then transferred the engines from the old aircraft into the new ones, with the old airframes mostly being scrapped.

During its relatively long service career, the F-101 fulfilled a range of different roles but was most successful as a reconnaissance platform. RF-101Cs serving during the Vietnam War flew faster than the F-4, F-8 or F-105 and their pilots relied on them to run a gauntlet of enemy fighters, anti-aircraft fire and SAMs. Despite failing to make much impact in the fighter role, the F-101 nevertheless managed to prove its worth. A total of 807 examples were built.●

McDONNELL F-101B-70-MC VOODOO ▽

McDonnell F-101B-70-MC Voodoo, 56-0271, 87th Fighter Interceptor Squadron, Lockbourne AFB, Columbus, Ohio. The 87th FIS operated the Voodoo from 1960 to 1968. The F-101B could carry AIM-4 Falcons in its weapons bay.

McDONNELL F-101B-105-MC VOODOO ▽

McDonnell F-101B-105-MC, 58-0259, 15th Fighter Interceptor Squadron, Davis Monthan AFB, Arizona, 1962. The 15th Fighter Interceptor Squadron operated the F-101B from 1960 to 1964 when it was disbanded. This aircraft is depicted as it appeared at Eglin AFB test range in 1983 in natural metal finish.

DURING ITS RELATIVELY LONG SERVICE CAREER, THE F-101 FULFILLED A RANGE OF DIFFERENT ROLES BUT WAS MOST SUCCESSFUL AS A RECONNAISSANCE PLATFORM.

McDONNELL F-101B

McDonnell F-101B, 58-0303, Air Defense Weapons Center, Tyndall Air Force Base, Florida, 1979-1981. The ADWC used its Voodoos to train crews in tactics and weapons.

80303

60271

80259

CONVAIR F-102

The delta-wing F-102A, commonly known as the 'Deuce' rather than by its official name, defended America's skies at a time when attack by Soviet bombers carrying nuclear weapons was still a very real possibility and as such earned its place in history.

A design competition to create a new advanced all-weather interceptor for the USAF commenced in January 1950 with the stipulations that the winning entry should be ready to fly in 1954 and should adhere to the 'weapon system' concept.

This meant that the new aircraft would be designed around a fire-control system (FCS), rather than an aircraft being built and then fitted with an FCS. The

USAF Air Material Command invited an incredible 50 companies to bid for the interceptor contract and 18 replied with designs which varied wildly both in form and cost.

Six aircraft manufacturers were shortlisted in May 1950 and at the same time Hughes beat rival North American to win the contract to develop the FCS – known as MX-1179.

Eventually, on July 2, 1951, it was announced that Republic, Lockheed

CONVAIR F-102A-45-CO DELTA DAGGER

Convair F-102A-45-CO, 55-3380, FC-380, 327th Fighter Interceptor Squadron, 1958. The F-102 entered operational service with the USAF with the 327th FIS, based at George Air Force Base in April 1956. This was the aircraft flown by the squadron's commander in 1958.

DELTA DAGGER

and Convair would each received a development contract to take their design as far as the mock-up stage. At this point Lockheed decided not to proceed with its bid, so just Convair and Republic went forward to mock-up construction with Convair being chosen as the winner and its futuristic-looking pure delta wing design receiving the designation XF-102.

By now it was clear that the Pratt & Whitney J57-powered XF-102 would be an interim interceptor, with a later version powered by the J67 – a derivation of the British-built Bristol Olympus – being the ultimate interceptor designated F-102B.

Meanwhile, Hughes was struggling with the MX-1179 and it was clear that the interim interceptor would have to be fitted with an interim FCS, known as the E-9.

CONVAIR F-102A-75-CO DELTA DAGGER

Convair F-102A-75-CO, 56-1333, FC-333, 318th Fighter Interceptor Squadron, McChord Air Force Base, Washington, 1958. Delta Daggers were the first supersonic aircraft flown by the 318th FIS, which operated them between 1957 and 1960. With the acceptance of these new fighters, a new insignia called 'Mach wave' was also adopted and displayed on the vertical fin.

Convair F-102 Delta Dagger

The completed YF-102 prototype made its first flight on October 23, 1953. Convair had decided to base its design on the XF-92A which it had begun working on as the XP-92 in 1946. This unusual arrowhead-shaped design was itself based on captured German Second World War aerodynamics research and in consultation with tailless and delta wing pioneer Alexander Lippisch – designer of the Messerschmitt Me 163 rocket-propelled interceptor.

It was thought that using existing research results and aerodynamics data would be a safe bet for the advanced YF-102 but unfortunately the aircraft's performance proved to be extremely disappointing in practice. It managed just six complete flights before being wrecked during its seventh on November 2, 1953, after suffering an engine flame-out on take-off – the result of a fuel system failure.

The second YF-102, which first flew on January 11, 1954, only confirmed that the wind tunnel tests made before the type's construction had been flawed – it struggled to go supersonic, only just managing to do so during a dive on January 27 with a speed of Mach 1.06. A further eight YF-102s followed, all of them suffering from the same performance problem. It was decided in May 1954 that the E-9 FCS was also insufficient and the improved E-10 was specified instead.

The USAF conditionally ordered 20 two-seater TF-102A trainers in July 1954 while Convair made some radical changes to the single seater's design. The result was the YF-102A, which made its maiden flight on December 20, 1954. This aircraft featured a reconfigured 7ft-longer 'wasp waist' fuselage, designed

according to the area rule principle, and went through the sound barrier with relative ease during its second flight on December 21. The YF-102A also had a much improved cockpit canopy and exhausts plus a new engine in the form of the J57-P-41.

Pilot's found that the YF-102A needed less runway to take off, could manage Mach 1.2 in level flight and had a superior high-altitude performance to that of the YF-102. Initial performance testing lasted until February 1955 when a second phase began. Eventually the test regime incorporated a total of four YF-102As.

What Convair called the first production example of the F-102A flew on June 24, 1955, but even though the 'Y' had been removed, this aircraft was not yet a fully functioning 'weapon system'. It suffered from flutter above ▶

CONVAIR F-102A-41-CO DELTA DAGGER ⬛

Convair F-102A-41-CO, 55-3379, 509th Fighter Interceptor Squadron, Da Nang AB, South Vietnam, 1964. F-102s were deployed to Vietnam and among their roles in-theatre was air-to-ground attack. For such missions the aircraft were fitted with rockets carried on the fuselage bay doors, although this change of operational role was of limited success. The aircraft were painted in a South-East Asia colour scheme.

CONVAIR F-102A-90-CO DELTA DAGGER

Convair F-102A-90-CO, 57-0825, FC-825, 329th Fighter Interceptor Squadron, George Air Force Base, California, 1959. The 329th FIS accepted its first F-102 in 1958 and used the type for two years, before replacing it with the F-106 Delta Dart. AIM-4 Falcon air-to-air missiles were carried on the fuselage bay; in this image it is possible to see them with the bay doors open.

CONVAIR F-102A-75-CO DELTA DAGGER

Convair F-102A-75-CO, 56-1418, 57th Fighter Interceptor Squadron, Keflavik AB, Iceland, 1972. The 57th FIS assumed the air defence of Iceland for several decades, from 1954 to 1995, when it was stood down. It flew F-102s from 1962 to 1973.

CONVAIR F-102A-41-CO DELTA DAGGER

Convair F-102A-41-CO, 55-3377, FC-377, 16th Fighter Interceptor Squadron, Naha Air Base, Japan, 1960. Operating the F-102 for 12 years, the 16th FIS was based in Japan and deployed to several locations during this period, from Norway, to Turkey, to South Korea and beyond.

Convair F-102 Delta Dagger

0-62317

CONVAIR TF-102A-38-CO DELTA DAGGER

Convair TF-102A-38-CO, 56-2317, Air Defense Weapons Center, Tyndall AFB, Texas, 1968. The centre used its Delta Daggers for lead-in and weapons training of F-102 crews.

Mach 1.2 and extensive testing resulted in a host of changes to the aircraft's intakes which enabled the aircraft to reach Mach 1.5 without problems by January 1956.

The 23rd F-102A was experimentally fitted with a larger 11ft 6in fin – compared to the original 8ft 8in fin which was very similar to that of the XF-92A – and this became part of the production model's design following a series of further tests.

After years of expensive development, the F-102A finally entered operational service two years late in April 1956 with the 327th Fighter Interceptor Squadron.

While the F-102A's primary responsibility was the defence of

the continental United States from aerial attack, the type did see limited deployment overseas. Two squadrons were stationed in West Germany by mid-1959 – the number gradually increasing to six. During the build-up to Vietnam, the F-102A equipped five fighter squadrons of the Pacific Air Forces and Operation Water Glass saw a quartet of F-102As from the 509th Fighter-Interceptor Squadron stationed at Tan Son Nhut air base near Saigon from March 21, 1962.

The F-102As were tasked with intercepting incursions from the north by small unidentified aircraft flying slowly at treetop height – a mission for which they were extremely ill-suited, having been

designed to tackle fast Soviet bombers at high altitude. These were later swapped for TF-102s since it was felt that having one of the two pilots functioning solely as a radar operator would improve the chances of a successful intercept.

This continued until May 1963 before being revived in November 1963 under the new name Operation Candy Machine. When American involvement in Vietnam escalated, F-102As were tasked with providing air defence for US bases, conducting ground-attack missions using rockets and escorting bombers but the type failed to shoot down a single enemy aircraft. Fifteen F-102As were lost in Vietnam though – seven in accidents or

CONVAIR TF-102A-35-CO DELTA DAGGER

Convair TF-102A-35-CO, 55-4045, TC-045, 431st Fighter Interceptor Squadron, Zaragoza AB, Spain, 1958-1964. While equipped with the F-102, the 431st was based in Spain and assigned to the 86th Air Division, part of USAFE. TF-102s were the conversion type and the operational squadron had some examples integrated.

THE F-102As WERE TASKED WITH INTERCEPTING INCURSIONS FROM THE NORTH BY SMALL UNIDENTIFIED AIRCRAFT FLYING SLOWLY AT TREETOP HEIGHT.

61032

S. AIR FORCE FC-032

as a result of mechanical failure, three being hit by ground fire, four destroyed on the ground in a Viet Cong mortar attack, and one actually being shot down by a MiG-21 using an AA-2 Atoll missile.

The F-102A continued to serve with the USAF and Air National Guard units well into the 1970s. Starting in 1973, hundreds of surviving F-102As were converted for use as target drones under the designation QF-102A and shot down by F-4s, F-106s and F-15s. Some were even used to test the Patriot missile system for the US Army.

A small number of F-102As and TF-102As were exported to

Turkey and Greece, who both retired them in 1979. The type had left US service in 1976 and the last QF-102A was shot down in 1986. A total of 889 F-102As were built.●

61009

E FC-009

CONVAIR F-102A-55-CO DELTA DAGGER

Convair F-102A-55-CO, 56-1032, FC-032, 32nd Fighter Interceptor Squadron, Soesterberg AB, Netherlands, 1964. Part of USAFE, the 32nd FIS displays the Crown and Wreath of the Royal House of Orange on its squadron badge as a recognition of its contribution to the defence of the Netherlands.

CONVAIR F-102A-55-CO DELTA DAGGER

Convair F-102A-55-CO, 56-1009, FC-009, 48th Fighter Interceptor Squadron, Langley Air Force Base, Virginia, 1958. The 48th FIS assumed the air defence of areas around the United States capital, being assigned to the Washington Air Defense Sector, Air Defense Command.

54045

U. S. AIR FORCE TC-045

LOCKHEED F-10

The slender short-winged F-104 offered staggering performance as an interceptor and also served in the reconnaissance, nuclear bomber and ground-attack roles – but also developed a reputation as a 'widow maker' thanks to unenviable litany of fatal accidents.

Lockheed's design team started work on what would become the F-104 in March 1952. The USAF's WS-303A weapon system requirement had called for a new high-speed tactical day fighter with the ability to go supersonic in level flight and Lockheed's Kelly Johnson decided that a lightweight design was the best way to achieve maximum performance.

After studying a host of different configurations, the basic outline of the finished aircraft was established in November 1952. The Lockheed L-246, also known as the Model 83, was submitted to the USAF in early 1953. The aircraft's remarkably short, unswept and incredibly thin wing form was based on Lockheed's experience with the X-7 unmanned ramjet test vehicle combined with extensive wind tunnel testing. Famously, the F-104's wing leading edge

1956-1968

LOCKHEED F-104A-15-LO STARFIGHTER

Lockheed F-104A-15-LO Starfighter, 56-0788, FG-788, 83rd Fighter Interceptor Squadron, Hamilton Air Force Base, California, 1958. The first USAF unit to become operational with the F-104A was the 83rd Fighter Interceptor Squadron in 1958.

4 STARFIGHTER

had a radius of just 0.016in and therefore required a protective cover to prevent ground crew from being injured by it.

The USAF ordered a pair of XF-104 prototypes in March 1953 and the first one took to the air briefly on February 28, 1954, before making a full flight on March 4. Like the second prototype which soon followed, it was powered by an interim engine – Curtiss-Wright's version of the British Armstrong Siddeley Sapphire jet, the XJ65-W-6. This produced 7200lb of thrust or 10,200lb with afterburner.

Johnson's decision to keep weight down paid off dramatically: despite its relative lack of power the prototypes proved capable of Mach 1.79.

A series of 17 pre-production YF-104As came next with deliveries commencing on February 17, 1956. These were powered by the engine the F-104 had been designed for – the

General Electric J79-GE-3A with 9600lb of trust or 14,800lb with afterburner. This necessitated a wider and longer rear fuselage but the YF-104A also featured a taller fin, a forwards rather than rearwards retracting nosewheel, a new spine and variable air intakes with a central shock cone and internal bleed slot.

The combination of these features enabled the F-104 to top Mach 2 in level flight – making it the first production model fighter with that capability. A YF-104A first topped Mach 2 on April 27, 1955, and the USAF then placed an order for 146 F-104As. The 'A' featured a new ventral fin under the rear fuselage and in-flight refuelling equipment.

The order was increased to 153 examples in October 1956 plus orders for 18 RF-104A reconnaissance variants, 56 F-104C fighter-bombers and 26 F-104B two-seat trainers. The first example of the

latter made its initial flight on February 7, 1957, and the first examples of both types began to enter USAF service in early 1958. Captain Walter W. Irwin, flying a YF-104A, broke the world air speed record on May 18, 1958, at 1399.79mph.

Unfortunately, the early J79 engine was unreliable and 21 pilots lost their lives testing the F-104. And the aircraft's unusual Lockheed-designed ejection seat, which fired the pilot down through the fuselage, failed to save them. After just a few months in service the F-104A was grounded due to concerns about its mechanical issues and poor handling in flight. In addition, the afterburner could not be regulated so pilots has a choice of flying at Mach 1 without afterburner or Mach 2.2 with afterburner and nothing in between.

The RF-104A order was cancelled in 1957 but the F-104C order went ahead. ▶

LOCKHEED F-104A-20-LO STARFIGHTER

Lockheed F-104A-20-LO Starfighter, 56-0824, FG-824, 331st Fighter Interceptor Squadron, Webb Air Force Base, Texas, 1964. The 331st FIS deployed its Starfighters to Taiwan in September 1958, during the so-called Second Taiwan Strait Crisis.

USAF FIGHTERS Lockheed F-104 Starfighter

LOCKHEED F-104C-5-LO STARFIGHTER ▲

Lockheed F-104C-5-LO Starfighter, 56-0891, FG-891, *Really George*, 479th Tactical
Fighter Wing, Nellis Air Force Base, Nevada, 1958. Undoubtedly one of the most colourful
Starfighters in USAF service, FG-891 is depicted as it appeared at the presentation of the
F-104C to the 479th TFW.

LOCKHEED F-104D-5-LO STARFIGHTER ▽

Lockheed F-104D-5-LO Starfighter, 57-1315,
FG-315, Air Force Flight Test Center, Edwards
Air Force Base, California, 1960. Twenty-one
dual-seat D models were delivered to the
USAF. FG-315 was assigned to the AFFTC
and was used in a variety of tests.

The 'C' had a conventional ejection
seat as standard and was designed to
drop tactical nuclear weapons. A trainer
version of the 'C', the F-104D, was
ordered in 1957.

Deliveries of the F-104C began in
October 1958. However, lack of faith in
the early F-104 design was so great that
the F-104As were withdrawn from USAF
service in 1959 and transferred to the Air
National Guard. The crashes continued
until by April 1961 a total of 49 F-104s
had been destroyed in accidents. Total
USAF orders for the F-104, excluding
prototypes, amounted to 294 airframes.
This figure comprised 170 F-104As, 26
F-104Bs, 77 F-104Cs and 21 F-104Ds.

In 1963, the USAF took enough

F-104As back from the ANG for two
squadrons and kept these in service until
December 1969. F-104Cs saw action in
Vietnam but the type was phased out
entirely in early 1968.

While the F-104 was not particularly
successful as a USAF fighter, it would
also be operated by Belgium, Canada
– where it was built under licence as
the CF-104 – Denmark, West Germany,
Greece, Italy – where the F-104S was
built under licence – Japan, Jordan, the
Netherlands, Norway, Pakistan, Spain,
Taiwan and Turkey.

The F-104 would also enjoy a
successful career as a testbed with
NASA, with 12 examples being flown
between 1956 and 1994.●

THE 'C' HAD A CONVENTIONAL EJECTION SEAT AS STANDARD AND WAS DESIGNED TO DROP TACTICAL NUCLEAR WEAPONS.

LOCKHEED F-104C-10-LO STARFIGHTER

Lockheed F-104C-10-LO Starfighter, 57-0923, *Hellooo Dolly*, 479th Tactical Fighter Wing, Udorn Royal Thai Air Force Base, Thailand 1966. Deployed to the Vietnam War, Starfighters received a South-East Asia camouflage scheme.

LOCKHEED F-104C-5-LO STARFIGHTER

Lockheed F-104C-5-LO Starfighter, 56-0923, FG-923, 436th Tactical Fighter Squadron, George Air Force Base, California, 1960. FG-923 was the squadron commander's aircraft; it carries ventral dual-sidewinder missile rails.

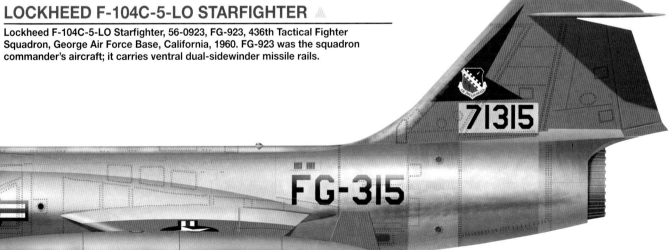

75792

REPUBLIC F-105 THUNDERCHIEF

The largest single engined fighter yet built when it entered service, the F-105 Thunderchief – or 'Thud' as it was more commonly known – came into its own flying low over the jungles of Vietnam.

Following on from the relative success of the F-84 family, starting in 1951 Republic ploughed its own funds into the development of a successor – a fighter-bomber capable of carrying a nuclear payload at speeds of up to Mach 1.5. The company called its new

1955-1984

10163

U.S. AIR FORCE

REPUBLIC F-105B-15-RE THUNDERCHIEF

Republic F-105B-15-RE Thunderchief, 57-5792, 335th Tactical Fighter Squadron, 4th Tactical Fighter Wing, Seymour Johnson Air Force Base, North Carolina, 1959. The F-105B entered USAF service with the Tactical Air Command in August 1958, although the first squadron did not become fully operational until 1959.

design Advanced Project 63 Fighter Bomber Experimental or 'AP-63FBX'.

After discussions with the USAF a formal proposal was submitted by the company in April 1952. Within a month, the air force had given the company license to proceed and a full contract for 199 aircraft was issued in September. Six months later, however, this was slashed back to just 37 of the original fighter-bomber and nine of the reconnaissance version.

The AP-63FBX was to be armed with four T-130 0.6in guns and powered by a single Allison J71 turbojet. It would have an MA-8 fire control system which included an AN/APG-31 radar, K-19 sight, flight computer and T-145 stores release system.

A mock-up was examined in October 1953 and received official approval. The type was then given the designation

F-105A but to Republic's horror, the whole contract was cancelled in December 1953. After strong protestations from the company – which had refused to give up on the design and continued to develop it even without a contract – an even more truncated order was issued in February 1954 for just 15 prototype examples. By now the F-105's shape had largely been finalised and the four 0.6in guns had been replaced with a single General Electric T-171D 20mm rotary cannon.

Work on the project proceeded but after seven months of painstaking development work Republic was once again hit by the news that the number of aircraft required had been reduced – down to three aircraft in September 1954. Then back up to six in October and then 15 again in February 1955.

▶

REPUBLIC F-105D-15-RE THUNDERCHIEF

Republic F-105D-15-RE Thunderchief, 61-0093, 9th Tactical Fighter Squadron, Spangdahlem Air Base, West Germany, 1963. The F-105D entered service with the 335th Tactical Fighter Squadron in September 1960, achieving full operational status in early 1961. Units operating in West Germany (36th and 49th Tactical Fighter Wings) had a primarily tactical nuclear role within NATO. The F-105 could carry a nuclear bomb on the weapons bay and the aircraft shown here is carrying a B43 in a semi-retracted position.

REPUBLIC F-105D-25-RE THUNDERCHIEF

Republic F-105D-25-RE Thunderchief, 61-0163, 562nd Tactical Fighter Squadron, McConnell Air Force Base, Kansas, 1965. The 562nd TFS was deployed to Takhli Royal Thai Air Force Base in 1965.

Republic F-105 Thunderchief

REPUBLIC F-105D-20-RE THUNDERCHIEF ▽

Republic F-105D-20-RE Thunderchief, 61-0139, 334th Tactical Fighter Squadron, Takhli
Royal Thai Air Force Base, Thailand 1966. Due to an increase in enemy fighter activity, when
operating over Vietnam F-105s were equipped with AIM-9 Sidewinders for self-defence.

This waxing and waning of interest in the F-105 was largely down to the rapid pace of technological advancement which characterised the era. The original Republic proposal lacked features which the USAF quickly realised it couldn't do without and in December 1954 the company was asked to make three very specific changes to the F-105. Firstly, the aircraft would have to be capable of in-flight refuelling. Secondly, it needed to make use of an advanced fire control system. And thirdly, the original calculated performance of the F-105 was sub-par. The USAF demanded a big improvement in speed.

The J71 was never going to yield the necessary increase in speed so in April 1955 it was swapped for the Pratt & Whitney J75-P-3 – rated at 23,500lb of thrust with afterburning, an increase of 8000lb on the J71. However, delays in development of the J75 meant that the first two YF-105A prototypes were fitted with a J57 instead.

The first prototype began flight testing on October 22, 1955, and went through the sound barrier on the same day. But it was clear that the YF-105A was still lacking in performance and the aircraft

REPUBLIC F-105D-31-RE THUNDERCHIEF ▽

Republic F-105D-31-RE Thunderchief, 62-4367, 354th Tactical Fighter Squadron, Takhli
Royal Thai Air Force base, Thailand, 1968. Thunderchiefs were equipped with a range of
air-to-ground weapons, including some missiles types. The AGM-12 Bullpup was used
with mixed results in the Vietnam conflict.

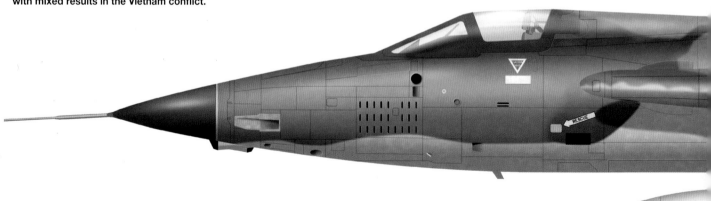

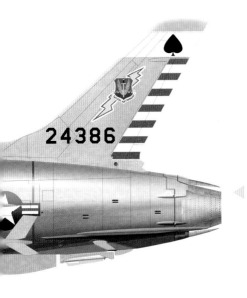

24386

REPUBLIC F-105D-31-RE THUNDERCHIEF

Republic F-105D-31-RE Thunderchief, 62-4386, 563rd Tactical Fighter Squadron, 23rd Tactical Fighter Wing, McConnell Air Force Base, Kansas 1965. The 563rd TFS was deployed to Takhli Royal Thai Air Force Base in 1965.

REPUBLIC F-105D-31-RE THUNDERCHIEF

Republic F-105D-31-RE Thunderchief, 62-4284, 354th Tactical Fighter Squadron, 355th Tactical Fighter Wing, 1967. 62-4284 displays three MiG kill markings, representing a double kill by Captain Max C. Brestel on March 10, 1967, and one from Captain Gene I. Basel on October 27, 1967. All three kills were MiG-17s.

was plagued by mechanical problems. The second prototype took to the air for the first time on January 28, 1956, but suffered from the same maladies as its sibling. The first YF-105A was destroyed in a crash in March and the second in a crash-landing not long afterwards.

The third prototype, which first flew on May 26, 1956, was substantially different from the first two. It finally had the specified J75 engine, new forward-swept air intakes incorporating adjustable ramps and perhaps most significantly a fuselage which had the curved area-rule form in place of the original's slab sides.

This new F-105, the F-105B, was now capable of Mach 2 albeit at a cost of increased tail flutter – this being overcome with the introduction of an enlarged tail surface. The F-105B also got ▶

Republic F-105 Thunderchief

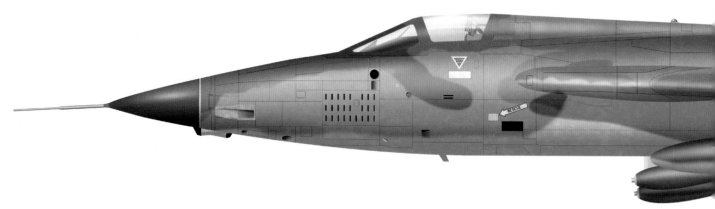

REPUBLIC F-105D-5-RE THUNDERCHIEF

Republic F-105D-5-RE Thunderchief, 59-1729, 333rd Tactical Fighter Squadron, 355th Tactical Fighter Wing, Takhli Royal Thai Air Force Base, Thailand, 1969. This aircraft was painted in a 'reverse' camouflage colour scheme; it carries an AN/ALQ-71 ECM pod on the outer wing pylon.

four-petal air brakes which fitted around the jet exhaust and the small cockpit canopy rear window seen on the earliest F-105 airframes was deleted.

Following its first flight, the prototype F-105B's landing gear would not extend so it had to be crash-landed. But the damage caused was not severe and the aircraft was returned to flight-ready status six weeks later. A planned reconnaissance version, the RF-105B, was cancelled in July 1956 and a two-seater version designated F-105C was cancelled in 1957 just as a mock-up was being readied for examination.

The production model F-105B – with the same designation as four prototype airframes which had precede it – was accepted into USAF service in August 1958 with the 335th Tactical Fighter Squadron.

Republic had continued to refine the F-105 design, however, and in 1958 had offered the USAF a much improved version with a more advanced fire control system, a more powerful engine and a far better instrument display based on experience with the earlier F-105s. It was also armed with the remarkable General Electric M61A1 Vulcan rotary cannon. The air force was so impressed with this new proposal that it quickly ordered 1500 examples of the aircraft – the F-105D. A two-seater version, the F-105E, was also planned but cancelled on March 18, 1959.

The first F-105D was completed in May 1959 and flown on June 9, 1959. Everything went smoothly for a change and the F-105D began to enter USAF service in May 1960, once again with the 335th. Yet Republic suffered another misfortune when Secretary of Defense Robert McNamara decided that the

superior all-round performance of the new F-4 Phantom II meant that only 750 Thunderchiefs would be needed – and the production order was cut accordingly.

However, as more and more units were equipped with the F-105D it became clear that a two-seat trainer version was essential. The F-105 was not an easy aircraft to fly and it was too big a jump from the T-33 up to the F-105D. As a result, Republic received an order for the F-105F, which was essentially an F-105D

with a stretched forward fuselage, providing accommodation for a second pilot. The 'back-seater' received a set of controls which almost exactly duplicated those at the front, which meant either pilot could operate all of the aircraft's systems.

The first 'F' rolled off the Republic production line on May 23, 1963, and first flew on June 11. Deliveries commenced on December 7 – just in time. F-105 units were among the first USAF forces

REPUBLIC F-105F-1-RE THUNDERCHIEF

Republic F-105F-1-RE Thunderchief, 63-8321, 357th Tactical Fighter Squadron, 355th Tactical Fighter Wing, Takhli Royal Thai Air Force Base, Thailand 1969. Some F-105F were modified into dedicated Wild Weasel aircraft and ability to fire the AGM-45 Shrike anti-radiation missile was a major improvement when attacking SAM sites, compared to the earlier method of using unguided bombs and rockets.

REPUBLIC F-105D-10-RE, 60-0471

Republic F-105D-10-RE, 60-0471, 457th Tactical Fighter Squadron, Air Force Reserve, Carswell Air Force Base, Texas, 1972. To improve navigation and precision targeting performance, several F-105Ds were modified to accommodate upgraded avionics in a larger dorsal spine. These modified aircraft were known as Thundersticks.

REPUBLIC F-105F-1-RE THUNDERCHIEF

Republic F-105F-1-RE Thunderchief, 63-8280, 35th Tactical Fighter Squadron, 8th Tactical Fighter Wing, Yokota Air Base, Japan, 1964. Dual-seat F-101Fs retained the combat capability of the single seat variant.

deployed to Vietnam in 1964 following the Gulf of Tonkin incident but the aircraft initially struggled with the hot and humid climate of South East Asia. Small air scoops were retrofitted to the rear fuselage to draw cooling air into the aircraft's afterburner to prevent an intolerable heat build-up. In addition, it was discovered that the F-105's hydraulic system was acutely vulnerable to combat damage and various measures were introduced to improve survivability including a third redundant hydraulic system.

As the conflict escalated, a need arose for a 'Wild Weasel' aircraft capable of countering the threat of North Vietnamese surface-to-air missile systems. The F-100F was initially chosen but the F-105F proved more suitable and the first adapted airframe, known as the EF-105F within the air force, was ready on January 16, 1966. It was packed with radar homing and warning electronics for detecting and identifying SAM and AAA sites. And it was armed with a fearsome arsenal of gravity bombs, rocket pods, napalm and AGM-45 Shrike anti-radar missile for knocking them out.

'Wild Weasel' was a highly dangerous mission which involved the EF-105s flying ahead of a strike force and effectively offering themselves up for any enemy ground defences. Once an enemy radar system was activated it would be a case of trying to destroy it before the EF-105 itself was destroyed.

Another product of the Vietnam War was the F-105G – a modification made to 61 existing F-105F airframes. Each aircraft was fitted with the Search, Exploit and Evade Surface to Air Missile Systems system or 'SEESAMS' for short, which improved on the EF-105's radar detection capabilities, and built-in electronic countermeasures equipment. These first Gs entered the war in late 1970.

By now the F-105's days were numbered. Just 833 examples had been built and a total of 395 had been lost during the war – 296 F-105Ds and 38 F-105F/Gs had been destroyed by enemy action and another 61 of all types due to accidents and mechanical failures.

By 1974 the only F-105s still in active operational service were EF-105Fs and F-105Gs, although some F-105Ds were still flown by the Air Force Reserve, and the last official F-105 flight took place on February 25, 1984.

Constantly under threat from shifting military requirements and political decisions, the F-105 somehow struggled through into active service but went on to show its true colours in the heat of combat – inspiring respect in its pilots and fear in its enemies.●

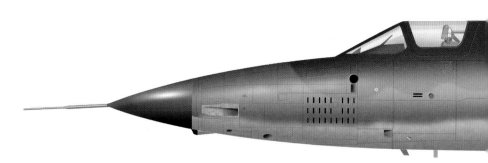

REPUBLIC F-105G-1-RE THUNDERCHIEF ▽

Republic F-105G-1-RE Thunderchief, 63-8275 Wild Weasel III, 17th Tactical Fighter Squadron, 388th Tactical Fighter Wing 1972. The G variant was a further development of the Thunderchief into a dedicated Wild Weasel platform, featuring improvements in both the avionics and weapons, including the AGM-78 Standard anti-radiation missile alongside with the AGM-45 Shrike.

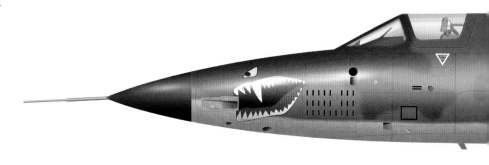

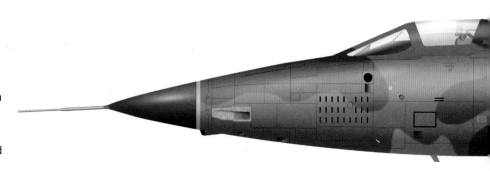

REPUBLIC F-105F-1-RE THUNDERCHIEF ▽

Republic F-105F-1-RE Thunderchief, 62-4444, 357th Tactical Fighter Squadron, 355th Tactical Fighter Wing, Takhli Royal Thai Air Force Base, Thailand 1969. Some F-105F airframes were modified through the Combat Martin programme, with the installation of communication jamming systems in the rear seat area. These modifications were intended to interfere with communications between ground control and the pilots of the North Vietnamese Air Force. Externally, the modified aircraft could easily be identified by a large antenna installed on the dorsal spine, just aft of the rear cockpit.

REPUBLIC F-105D-31-RE THUNDERCHIEF ▽

Republic F-105D-31-RE Thunderchief, 62-299, 466th Tactical Fighter Squadron, 419th Tactical Fighter Wing, USAF Air Force Reserve, 1983. The last units to fly the Thunderchief were from the Air Force Reserve. The aircraft were finally retired from service between 1983 and 1984. The 466th TFS had aircraft painted in several unusual wraparound colour schemes.

CONVAIR F-106

The F-102 was designed as the USAF's 1954 interceptor but it arrived two years late and fell short of expectations as the 'ultimate' interceptor. That title went to the F-106 – which had begun life as the F-102B.

T he F-102B was to be an F-102A fitted with the more powerful J75 engine in place of its J57 so it could tackle the next generation of Soviet bombers such as the Myasishchev M-4 'Bison' which had come to American attention during the 1954 Mayday parade in Red Square.

The USAF was initially hesitant about ordering the F-102B and Convair therefore made a concerted effort to sell it to the US Navy as a high-altitude

1956–1988

60467

FE-467   U.S. AIR

CONVAIR F-106A-85-CO DELTA DART

Convair F-106A-85-CO, Delta Dart, 57-2478, 498th Fighter Interceptor Squadron, Geiger Field, Washington, 1959. The Delta Dart was introduced into operational USAF service with the 498th FIS, the famous Geiger Tigers.

DELTA DART

carrier-based interceptor. The navy version would have been powered by either the J67 or the J75 and armed with four AIM-7A Sparrow missiles or six AIM-9 Sidewinders (though neither missile was yet known by those later designations).

Strengthened wings and landing gear, a small tailhook and a folding fin tip were also incorporated into the design. However, the US Navy declined the proposal and the USAF decided in favour

of having its own F-102B. A contract for 17 examples was given to Convair in November 1955 and a full production order followed on April 18, 1956. In less than a month, the aircraft had been given a new designation to differentiate it from its predecessor – F-106A. A two-seat version was ordered as the TF-106A on August 3, 1956, and this too had received a new designation by the end of that month – F-106B.

The F-106's wing was derived from

that of the F-102A but its fuselage was significantly different. Its overall shape was more steamlined and the air intakes for its engines – which had been positioned on either side of the cockpit on the F-102 – were now much closer to the engine itself. The cockpit was closer to the tip of the aircraft's nose but the pilot sat well back from the windscreen. Some early F-106s had an additional fuel tank built into their fin but this feature was later deleted because it could play ▶

CONVAIR F-106A DELTA DART

Convair F-106A, 56-0467, FE-467, Air Force Flight Test Center, Edwards Air Force Base, California, 1959. Using this aircraft, Major Joe Rogers set a new world speed record of 1525mph on December 15, 1959.

CONVAIR F-106A-105-COV DELTA DART ▽

Convair F-106A-105-CO, Delta Dart, 59-0005, 5th Fighter Interceptor Squadron, Minot Air Force Base, North Dakota, 1961. The most potent weapons available to the Delta Dart was the nuclear air-to-air rocket, AIR-2 Genie; carried internally in its weapons bay – seen here partially extended in readiness for launch.

havoc with the aircraft's centre of gravity if it failed to operate correctly.

The F-106A was fitted with the MX-1179 fire control system originally designed for the F-102A. This would manage the aircraft's intended armament of Douglas MB-1 Genie projectiles and AIM-4 Falcons, carried internally in an under-fuselage weapons bay. The MX-1179 was renamed MA-1 and tests using a prototype finally got under way in December 1956. The MA-1 comprised

an autopilot, navigation system, radar and computer all working together. It could be pre-programmed and updated during the flight via signals from ground stations.

Also in December, Convair was battling frantically to get the first F-106A prototype, naturally lacking a fire control system of any sort, airborne. In order to satisfy its contractual obligations, the aircraft needed to fly before the end of 1956.

Ground runs began on December 22 and the first flight took place on December 26 – although it had to be aborted after just 20 minutes owing to air turbine motor frequency fluctuation and jammed speed brakes. The second prototype followed the first into the flight testing programme on February 26, 1957. Testing was divided into six phases, the first of which simply assessed basic airworthiness.

The second, which took place between May 22 and June 29, 1957, assessed ▶

CONVAIR F-106A-75-CO DELTA DART ▽

Convair F-106A-75-CO, Delta Dart, 57-2465, 2nd Fighter Interceptor Squadron, Tyndall Air Force Base, Florida, 1973. The 2nd FIS operated the F-106 for only two years before it was redesignated as the 2nd Fighter Interceptor Training Squadron. It made the last USAF F-106 training flights in 1982.

CONVAIR F-106A-105-CO DELTA DART

Convair F-106A-105-CO, Delta Dart, 59-0051, 87th Fighter Interceptor Squadron, K.I. Sawyer Air Force Base, Michigan, 1976. The F-106 could carry four AIM-4 Falcons, including a mix of SARH AIM-4Fs and IR AIM-4Gs, internally.

90005

90051

S. AIR FORCE

CONVAIR F-106A-80-CO DELTA DART

Convair F-106A-80-CO, Delta Dart, 57-2473, 95th Fighter Interceptor Squadron, Andrews Air Force Base, 1970. Based at Andrews AFB, the 95th was one of the squadrons deployed to South Korea, following several incidents involving North Korean forces. It was stationed at Osan Air base from late 1969 to mid-1970.

0-72473

0-72465

AIR FORCE

Convair F-106 Delta Dart

performance, stability and handling. This resulted in minor changes to the aircraft's intake duct and major changes to the ejection seat. It also revealed that, as with the F-102 before it, performance was substantially inferior to what Convair had claimed it would be – Mach 1.8 in level flight rather than the Mach 2 it should have been. Test pilots also strongly criticised the cockpit layout.

While the lengthy and drawn-out process of testing of the F-106A continued, the first F-106B made its flight debut on April 9, 1958. It had been thought that the F-106B, with its fuselage extended to house a second cockpit in

tandem to the first, would be slower than the F-106A – but testing revealed that its performance almost matched that of the single seater. Testing also highlighted issues with the aircraft's ejection and fuel systems which would prove difficult to fully resolve.

The first USAF unit to receive the F-106 was the 539th Fighter-Interceptor Squadron, on May 30, 1959, with a second unit, the 498th FIS, receiving its first example on June 1. On October 31, 1959, Russia test pilot Colonel Georgi Mosolov broke the world air speed record flying a MiG-21 at 1484mph. Not to be outdone, the USAF took up the

challenge and on December 15, 1959, Major Joe W Rogers retook the record for America, flying an F-106A at 1525.95mph – Mach 2.36.

The capabilities of the aircraft's remarkable fire control system were amply demonstrated on March 30, 1960, when an F-106A was flown for nearly four hours from Edwards Air Force Base in California to Jacksonville, Florida, solely by its on board MA-1. Pilot Major Frank Forsyth was on board for the take-off and landing – the only parts of the journey that the MA-1 was unable to handle.

For combat, the MA-1 could be programmed with two modes of attack

CONVAIR F-106A-120-CO DELTA DART

Convair F-106A-120-CO, 59-0077, 49th Fighter Interceptor Squadron, Griffiss Air Force base, New York, 1975. In 1972, under Project Six Shooter, the F-106 gained the ability to optionally carry a gun pod housing a 20mm M61 Vulcan.

CONVAIR F-106A-105-CO DELTA DART ▶

Convair F-106A-105-CO, 59-0020, 84th Fighter Interceptor Squadron, Castle Air Force Base, California, 1976. The 84th FIS operated the Delta Dart from 1968 to 1981.

– lead collision, which involved attacking the target head-on, and auto pursuit, where the MA-1's autopilot would engage the target from the rear. The fire control system, with the autopilot handling the manoeuvring in conjunction with the radar and navigation system, would conduct the attack. All the pilot needed to do was choose the appropriate weapon and hold down the trigger. When all the right conditions were in place, the FCS would launch the missile.

Unfortunately, the early MA-1 was bedevilled by glitches which reduced its reliability and effectiveness. The existence of this highly advanced yet ▶

CONVAIR F-106A-125-CO DELTA DART

Convair F-106A-125-CO, 59-0090, 11th Fighter Interceptor Squadron, Duluth International Airport, Minnesota, 1965. Operating the Delta Dart from 1960 to 1968, the 11th FIS was deactivated on that year and its aircraft were passed to the 87th FIS.

Convair F-106 Delta Dart

CONVAIR F-106B-75-CO DELTA DART ▽

Convair F-106B-75-CO, 59-0158, 48th Fighter Interceptor Squadron,
Langley Air Force Base, Virginia, 1968. The two-seater F-106B retained
the operational capability of the single-seat variant.

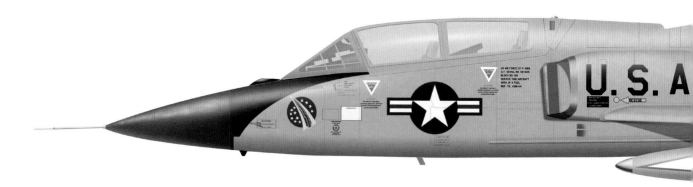

still rather simplistic system certainly encouraged the idea that the days of manned fighters were numbered and that the future of air warfare lay with guided missiles. With this in mind, the US Senate decided to cut funding for the F-106 beyond the first 340 and transferred the money to the Bomarc missile instead.

All F-106s were grounded on September 26, 1961, as problems with the aircraft's fuel system reached a head with two crashes and the death of a pilot. Urgent modifications were made across the fleet. The troublesome ejection seat,

however, remained a problem.

With the F-106s still grounded, the Pentagon launched a new competition between the US Navy F4H-1 Phantom II and the USAF's F-106A to determine which was better when they were called upon to perform the same missions. The USAF was looking to purchase 200 new fighters and was interested in the F4H-1.

Although the F-106 was said to have performed well during the competition, the F4H-1 with its better radar came out on top and was declared the winner after the content ended on November 17, 1961. No further F-106s were ordered.

The aircraft's ejection seat was finally replaced with a safer model during 1965 and on May 13, 1969, a pair of F-106s stationed at Loring Air Force Base, Maine, on the extreme north-eastern tip of the US, made the first interception of a Soviet bomber by a fighter launched from the continental United States. In this instance, they intercepted a trio of Tupolev Tu-95s after a lengthy pursuit.

Nearly two decades later, on August 1, 1988, the last official USAF F-106 flight took place when three aircraft from the 119th FIS took off from Atlantic City. Two years earlier, Flight Systems Inc. had

CONVAIR F-106A-100-CO DELTA DART ▽

Convair F-106A-100-CO, 58-0776, 318th Fighter Interceptor Squadron, McChord
Air Force Base, Washington, 1976. Nicknamed *The Freedom Bird*, this 318th FIS
aircraft was painted in a US Bicentenary commemorative scheme.

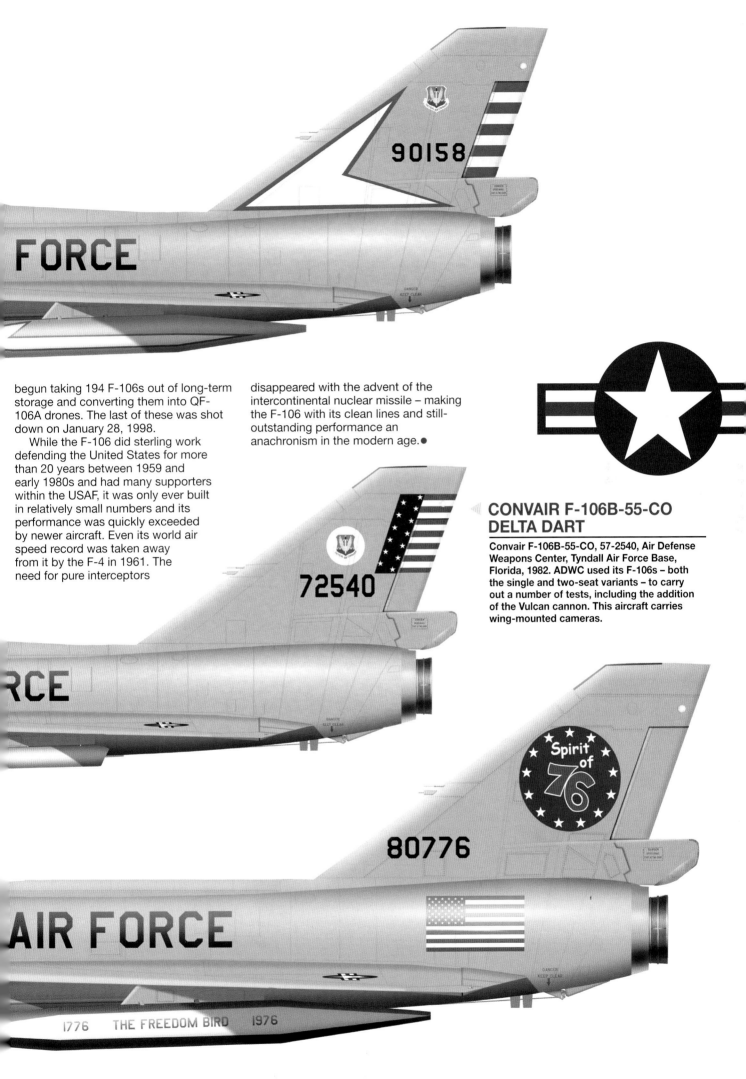

90158

FORCE

begun taking 194 F-106s out of long-term storage and converting them into QF-106A drones. The last of these was shot down on January 28, 1998.

While the F-106 did sterling work defending the United States for more than 20 years between 1959 and early 1980s and had many supporters within the USAF, it was only ever built in relatively small numbers and its performance was quickly exceeded by newer aircraft. Even its world air speed record was taken away from it by the F-4 in 1961. The need for pure interceptors

disappeared with the advent of the intercontinental nuclear missile – making the F-106 with its clean lines and still-outstanding performance an anachronism in the modern age.●

72540

RCE

CONVAIR F-106B-55-CO DELTA DART

Convair F-106B-55-CO, 57-2540, Air Defense Weapons Center, Tyndall Air Force Base, Florida, 1982. ADWC used its F-106s – both the single and two-seat variants – to carry out a number of tests, including the addition of the Vulcan cannon. This aircraft carries wing-mounted cameras.

Spirit of 76

80776

AIR FORCE

1776   THE FREEDOM BIRD   1976

McDONNELL DOUGLAS F-4 PHANTOM II

The Phantom surpassed its humble beginnings as an underpowered Navy interceptor to become one of the most capable and famous fighters of the postwar era. It was fast, reliable, adaptable and brutally powerful.

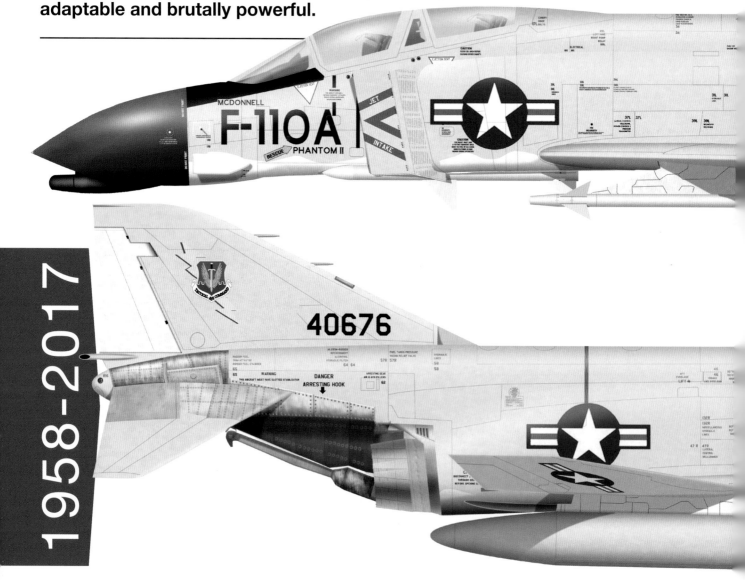

1958-2017

It became clear to the US Navy in early 1947 that it needed a high-performance jet-propelled interceptor capable of operating off a carrier deck. A request for proposals was issued to industry on May 21, 1948, and 11 aircraft designs were submitted for consideration. McDonnell's entry was the single-engined Model 58 and after seven months of comparisons and discussion was chosen for development under the designation F3H.

Construction of the first prototype suffered a series of delays due to difficulties with the Westinghouse J40 turbojet it had been designed around. McDonnell and Westinghouse were put under pressure to speed things up after American forces in Korea first encountered the fast and highly manoeuvrable swept-wing MiG-15 and the first XF3H-1 flew on August 1, 1951.

But the J40's problems were far from over and by now the US Navy had changed its requirement – the interceptor needed to have an all-weather capability. This meant it needed a radar and the ability to carry and fire guided missiles. The F3H, now given the name 'Demon', underwent a significant redesign. Although it was finally decided in November 1952 that the Allison J71 turbojet should take the J40's place, a batch of 58 production model F3H-1Ns was still built with the original engine. The first of these flew in December 1952 but after a series of fatal accidents, mostly due to the engine, they were grounded.

The J71-powered Demon had an enlarged wing and the first example flew on April 23, 1953. It was clear to McDonnell at this point, having gone through the pain of re-engining the Demon once, that the basic aerodynamic features of the aircraft were sound and could be adapted to suit a variety of engine configurations. A series of ▶

McDONNELL F-110A PHANTOM II

McDonnell F-110A Phantom II, 149405, St. Louis, Missouri, 1962.
Prior to the 1962 United States Tri-Service aircraft designation system, the Phantom had the USAF designation F-110A.

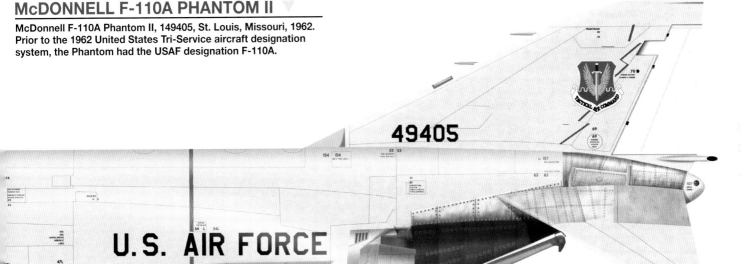

McDONNELL F-4C-22-MC PHANTOM II

McDonnell F-4C-22-MC Phantom II, 64-0676, 45th Tactical Fighter Squadron, Ubon Royal Thai Air Force Base, 1965. The first Phantoms to be deployed to the Vietnam theatre of operations carried a grey/white colour scheme.

McDonnell Douglas F-4 Phantom II

McDONNELL F-4C-24-MC PHANTOM II

McDonnell F-4C-24-MC Phantom II, 64-0840, 67th Tactical Fighter Squadron, 18th Tactical Fighter Wing, Korat Royal Thai Air Force Base, Thailand, 1972. Several F-4C were modified to carry out Wild Weasel missions; these aircraft were designated as EF-4C 'Wild Weasel IV' and carried an improved Radar Homing and Warning System (RHAWS), SAM launch warning systems and electronic countermeasures receivers. They were armed with anti-radiation missiles such as the AGM-45 Shrike depicted.

concept studies was launch in August 1953 – which consisted of the Demon fitted with a Wright J67, a pair of Wright J65s or a pair of General Electric J79s. In every case, the design had a larger wing than that of the F3H but other design details could be altered to suit: the aircraft could be a single or two-seater; it could be used for air-to-air interception or air-to-ground attack or reconnaissance; and it could carry a wide range of cannon, rockets or other stores.

An unsolicited proposal was made on September 19, 1953, and the Navy was sufficiently interested in the two twin-engine designs to order a mock-up in early 1954. This was duly produced and inspected on October 18, 1954, resulting in an order from the US Navy for two cannon-armed prototype single-seaters powered by twin J79s. However, this was altered to a pair of missile-armed two-seaters on May 26, 1955, under the designation YF4H-1. Two months later the order was expanded to five pre-production machines.

Armament was four AIM-7s in semi-recessed bays under the fuselage with an option to carry AIM-9s on underwing pylons. The cannon were deleted – making the YF4H-1 America's first missile-only fighter. The wings and engine intakes underwent extensive testing and redesign based on wind tunnel testing and the first prototype Phantom II made its maiden flight on May 27, 1958. After the aircraft won a fly-off against Vought's outlandish-looking XF8U-3 Crusader III in December 1958, the number on order was increased to 45.

After further testing, the aircraft's canopy was revised to improve pilot

McDONNELL F-4D-29-MC PHANTOM II

McDonnell F-4D-29-MC Phantom II, 66-0234, 435th Tactical Fighter Squadron, 8th Tactical Fighter Wing, Udorn Royal Thai Air Force Base, Thailand, 1972. The need for accurate bombing was felt early on during the Vietnam conflict but the introduction of missiles and laser guided bombs such as the GBU-10 dramatically improved the situation.

ARMAMENT WAS FOUR AIM-7S IN SEMI-RECESSED BAYS UNDER THE FUSELAGE WITH AN OPTION TO CARRY AIM-9S ON UNDERWING PYLONS.

visibility and a larger radome was installed to house the Westinghouse AN/APQ-72 radar's 32in dish. The intakes now had two ramps ahead of the duct, the first fixed and the second variable, and a retractable air refuelling probe was installed. A Texas Instruments AAA-4 infra-red sensor was fitted into a small pod beneath the radome to give the Phantom its now distinctive nose.

It was clear by now that the Phantom was an exceptional aircraft and US Secretary of Defense Robert S. McNamara directed the USAF

McDONNELL F-4D-29-MC PHANTOM II

McDonnell F-4D-29-MC Phantom II, 66-7463, 555th Tactical Fighter Squadron, of the 432nd Tactical Reconnaissance Wing, Udorn Royal Thai Air Force Base, Thailand, 1972. Captain Charles Barbin DeBellevue was the leading USAF ace of the Vietnam War. He achieved his fifth and sixth kills on September 9, 1972, operating as a WSO. All six kills were achieved during 1972.

McDonnell Douglas F-4 Phantom II

McDONNELL F-4E-35-MC PHANTOM II ◢

McDonnell F-4E-35-MC Phantom II, 67-0301, 469th Tactical Fighter
Squadron, 388th Tactical Fighter Wing, Korat Royal Thailand Air
Force Base, Thailand, 1969.

to consider the F4H-1F as its next
interceptor, fighter-bomber and
reconnaissance platform. During 1961,
as previously mentioned, the Phantom
was tested against the Convair F-106A,
Republic's F-105 Thunderchief and
McDonnell's own F-101 Voodoo for each
of those roles respectively.

While the USAF's response was
lukewarm at first, the tests soon
demonstrated that the Phantom really
was a next-generation machine. The
USAF version was ordered in January
1962 as the F-110A or RF-110A in
reconnaissance configuration. On
January 24, a pair of F4H-1s were sent
to Langley Air Force Base, Virginia, so
that Tactical Air Command could evaluate
them and in March the type was chosen
as TAC's new fighter and reconnaissance
aircraft for American forces in Europe and
the Pacific.

The Navy loaned the USAF a further
27 examples for testing and in September
1962, under the common designation
scheme, the F-110A was renumbered
F-4C and the RF-110A became the
RF-4C. The 'C' differed from the 'B' in
having full dual controls, more powerful
J79-GE-15 turbojets, a built-in cartridge
starting system, thicker low pressure
tyres for rough field use, a refuelling
receptacle in the upper fuselage instead
of the naval version's retractable probe
and an anti-skid undercarriage braking
system. It also had a different electronics

suite – the AN/APQ-100 radar, AN/ASN-
48 inertial navigation system and AN/
ASN-46 navigation computer – and it
could carry guided and unguided bombs,
AIM-4s, AIM-7s, rockets or gun pods.

The first USAF F-4C flew on May
27, 1963, and topped Mach 2 during
the flight. The USAF's first F-4Cs were
delivered in November 1963 to the
4453rd Combat Crew Training Wing and
the first front line unit to receive them
was the 12th Tactical Fighter Wing. The
F-4C saw extensive combat during the
Vietnam War – beginning with the 45th
Tactical Fighter Squadron's deployment
to Thailand in April 1965.

But just five months after the first
F-4Cs had been delivered, in March
1964, the air force ordered a new version
embodying further refinements to better
adapt the original naval design to USAF
operational requirements. The radar
was changed again, to the relatively
lightweight AN/APQ-109A, necessitating
a bigger radome, and the navigation
system was upgraded. The AN/ASG-
22 lead computing sight was fitted and ▶

McDONNELL YRF-4C, F-4C-14-MC PHANTOM II

McDonnell YRF-4C, F-4C-14-MC Phantom II, 62-12200, 1965. During the air war in Vietnam, the notion that fighters only needed missiles was disproved and the need for a gun was dramatically demonstrated. Initial tests involved the addition of the M61 Vulcan to the airframe of the YRF-4C. This aircraft was used in a variety of test programmes related to the Phantom and other aircraft.

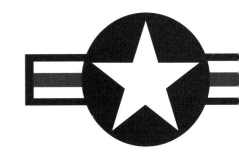

McDONNELL F-4E-32-MC PHANTOM II

McDonnell F-4E-32-MC Phantom II, 66-0300, 57th Fighter Interceptor Squadron, Keflavik, Iceland, 1985. The 57th FIS was responsible for the air defence of Iceland for several decades and Phantoms were among the last fighter types used by the unit. They were painted in an overall grey colour scheme.

McDONNELL F-4E-35-MC PHANTOM II

McDonnell F-4E-35-MC Phantom II, 67-0283, 469th Tactical Fighter Squadron, 388th Tactical Fighter Wing, Korat Royal Thailand Air Force Base, Thailand, 1972.

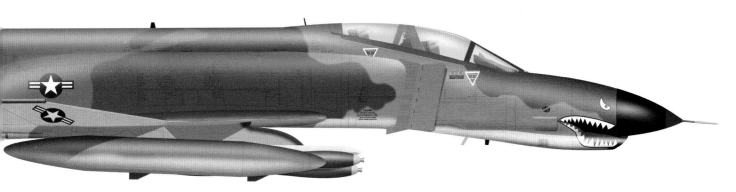

McDonnell Douglas F-4 Phantom II

McDonnell F-4E Phantom, number 4, Thunderbirds USAF Air Demonstration Squadron, Nellis Air Force Base, Nevada, 1970. The Thunderbirds used the Phantom from 1969 to 1973. Exhaust fumes from the team's other aircraft frequently blackened the tail of the number 4 aircraft.

the infra-red sensor was deleted then replaced with a radar sensor and SAM warning receiver. The 'D' would continue to be upgraded with additional sensor, targeting and other equipment throughout its long service career – allowing it to carry a wide range of weapons.

The F-4C and D feature that pilots were least enthusiastic about was its lack of a built-in cannon. McDonnell began considering how to address this in 1964 and by early 1965 had set about modifying the original YRF-4C prototype

with a longer nose to house a General Electric M61A1 20mm cannon – the radar having been moved forwards to make room. Redesignated YF-4E, the aircraft was first flown on August 7, 1965, and two further aircraft subsequently underwent the same modification, an F-4C and an F-4D, and a programme of trials commenced.

These proved successful and the air force placed an order for 96 production model F-4Es in August 1966. The production version differed from the

prototypes in having a slotted leading edge tailplane that had been developed for the naval F-4J and in deleting the wing folding mechanism that all earlier air force Phantoms had incorporated, in order to save weight. The engines were upgraded to J79-GE-17s and titanium sheeting was installed in the engine bays to mitigate the extra heat they produced. The radar was changed yet again to the AN/APQ-120 and a host of other associated electronics alterations were made. Like the F-4C's RF-4C

McDONNELL DOUGLAS F-4E-60-MC PHANTOM II

McDonnell Douglas F-4E-60-MC Phantom II, 74-048, 480th Tactical Fighter Squadron, Spangdahlem Air Base, West Germany, 1985.

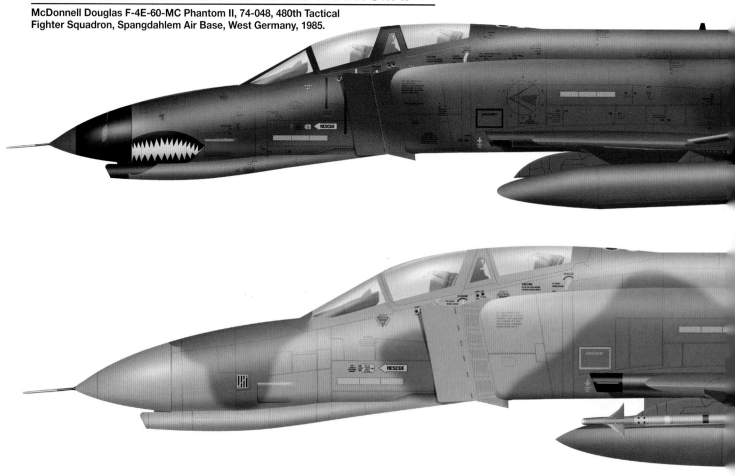

LIKE THE F-4C'S RF-4C RECONNAISSANCE VERSION, THERE WAS A CORRESPONDING RF-4E. THIS ESSENTIALLY INVOLVED GRAFTING THE FORMER'S CAMERA NOSE ONTO THE F-4E AIRFRAME.

AIR FORCE

reconnaissance version, there was a corresponding RF-4E. This essentially involved grafting the former's camera nose onto the F-4E airframe.

While the F-4F was a variant produced for West Germany, and therefore falls outside the scope of this publication, there were two different F-4Gs. The designation was first applied to 12 US Navy F-4Bs that were fitted with an AN/ASW-21 datalink communications system and other equipment associated with an automatic carrier landing system. The

first of these flew as early as March 20, 1963, and all 12 served aboard USS *Kitty Hawk* from November 1965 to June 1966, carrying out missions over Vietnam. One was lost in action and the remaining 11 were converted back to F-4B standard.

The USAF's F-4G, however, was the Wild Weasel version. The Wild Weasel mission, as previously mentioned, evolved during operations in Vietnam and involved aircraft fitted with complex electronics suites which enabled them ▶

McDONNELL DOUGLAS F-4E-60-MC PHANTOM II

McDonnell Douglas F-4E-60-MC Phantom II, 74-1040, 704th Tactical Fighter Squadron, 924th Tactical Fighter Group, Air Force Reserve, Bergstrom Air Force Base, Texas, 1991. Aircraft of this unit wore a colour scheme known as 'cloud'. This aircraft is equipped with the Target Identification System, Electro-Optical (TISEO).

to seek out and destroy the enemy's surface-to-air defence network. The Republic F-105F and the F-4C were modified for this role as the EF-105F and EF-4C.

The need for updated Wild Weasel aircraft remained after the Vietnam War and it was decided that the F-4E would provide the basis for the next generation SAM site killer. McDonnell Douglas – McDonnell having merged with Douglas Aircraft in 1967 – began testing modified F-4Es in December 1975. A total of 116 aircraft would eventually be modified under the designation F-4G.

The 'G' had its cannon nose removed and the space freed up was filled instead with sideways looking antenna and the AN/APR-38 warning and attack system. Further antenna for this system were mounted within a fairing on top of the aircraft's fin. The rear cockpit was extensively modified to house an electronic warfare officer with three screens to display sensor data, the radar screen, and the usual full dual controls.

The F-4G could carry most of the weapons used by earlier Phantoms if required but was also capable of firing AGM-88 HARM and TV or Imaging Infra Red versions of the AGM-75 Maverick missile. The first F-4Gs entered service in 1978 and another 18 F-4Es were converted to Gs in 1988 to replace losses. The type saw action during Operation Desert Storm in January and February 1991. The last examples were

retired from the Idaho Air National Guard in April 1996.

This was not the end of the American Phantom story however, with QF-4 drones remaining in service until January 1, 2017. A grand total of 5195 Phantoms were manufactured for all users – these including not only the USAF and US Navy but also air forces in the UK, Germany, Greece, Australia, Spain, Turkey, Japan, South Korea, Israel, Egypt and even, famously, Iran.

Thanks to its two-seater twin-engine layout, reliability, adaptability and capability the F-4 became the first truly modern jet fighter to serve with the USAF – the type remaining in service with many of its overseas customers 60 years after it first flew. The legendary fighter's story may have ended in the US but its legacy looks set to continue for years to come.●

McDONNELL DOUGLAS F-4G PHANTOM II ▽

McDonnell Douglas F-4G Phantom II, 69-7216, 561st Tactical Fighter Squadron, Sheikh Isa Air Base, Bahrain 1991. 'Wild Weasel Vs' were deployed to the Middle East to provide SAM protection for attack packages during Operation Desert Storm.

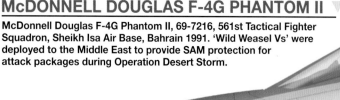

McDONNELL F-4E-41-MC PHANTOM II

McDonnell F-4E-41-MC Phantom II, 68-0506 512th Tactical Fighter Squadron, Ramstein Air Base, West Germany, 1983. Two aircraft of the 512th TFS were painted with conspicuous dragon mouths, reflecting the squadron's emblem and nickname. The aircraft is painted in a wraparound variant of the South-East Asia colour scheme.

McDONNELL DOUGLAS F-4E PHANTOM II

McDonnell Douglas F-4E Phantom II, 3rd Tactical Fighter Squadron, Incirlik Air Base, Turkey, 1991. Aircraft from the Philippines based (Clark Air Base) 3rd TFS squadron were deployed to Incirlik during the Desert Shield/Desert Storm operations.

McDONNELL DOUGLAS RF-4C-40-MC PHANTOM II

McDonnell Douglas RF-4C-40-MC Phantom II, 68-0597, 14th Tactical Reconnaissance Squadron, Udorn Royal Thai Air Force Base, Thailand, 1972. RF-4Cs played a vital role in Vietnam – combining a sophisticated reconnaissance package with a high-performance aircraft.

GENERAL DYNAMICS F-111 AARDVARK

U.S. AIR FORCE

Designed as a compromise between competing USAF and US Navy requirements, the F-111 ended up pleasing neither service. It was big, heavy, powerful and produced in only small numbers yet it did introduce cutting edge technology and enjoyed a respectable career.

1964-1998

USAF 66-018

When Francis Gary Powers' Lockheed U-2 spy plane was shot down by an SA-2 Guideline missile on May 1, 1960, the US realised that the Soviets had developed the capability to reliably hit targets flying above 60,000ft. But SAMs remained unable to hit targets flying very fast at extremely low level. Therefore, in June 1960, the USAF issued a specification for a long-range high-speed low-altitude strike aircraft able to operate from rough short airstrips.

At the same time, the US Navy was looking for a long-range fleet defence fighter with a more powerful radar than could be fitted to the

Phantom II. Having already compelled the USAF to take the Navy's F-4, Secretary of Defense McNamara ordered that both requirements be merged into the Tactical Fighter Experimental (TFX) programme. The two services could only agree on the need for two seats, two engines and a swing-wing configuration for improved take-off performance – but beyond that they had very different requirements.

The Navy wanted the crew to sit side-by-side so they could both see the radar screen but the USAF wanted a tandem arrangement for low-level strike missions. The Navy was happy with subsonic low level performance but the USAF needed Mach 1.2 at low altitude. And the Navy wanted a nose big enough to house a 48in radar dish.

A halfway house set of requirements that no one was happy with was drawn up and a request for proposals was made in October 1961. Six projects were put forward and those of Boeing and General Dynamics were chosen to proceed.

Both submitted updated proposals in April 1962 and the Boeing design was chosen as the winner by the official selection board. However, McNamara overruled this decision and decided to proceed with the General Dynamics design instead because it offered greater commonality between the Air Force and Navy versions. A contract was finally issued in December 1962 and General Dynamics commenced detailed design work on what was designated the F-111 – the F-4 having originally been the F-110.

The F-111A and F-111B were the USAF and US Navy versions respectively. Both had the same variable-sweep wing technology, allowing just 16° sweepback for take-off, landing and low speed operations and a 72.5° sweepback for high-speed flight. They also shared the same Pratt & Whitney TF30-P-1 turbofan engines, internal weapons bay, tricycle undercarriage and side-by-side seating for the two crew in an escape capsule cockpit.

The latter's nose was 8½ft shorter so that it would fit existing aircraft carrier elevators and had 3½ longer wingtips to improve endurance. The former was equipped with the innovative Texas Instruments AN/APQ-110 terrain-following radar as part of its electronics package.

An inspection of the F-111A mockup was made in September 1963 and the first example – with ejection seats rather than the production model's escape capsule – was completed on October 15, 1964. Its first flight was made on December 21, 1964, and it achieved

GENERAL DYNAMICS F-111A

General Dynamics F-111A, 63-9766, Air Force Flight Test Center, Edwards Air Force Base, California, 1964. The first prototype for the F-111A made its flight debut in December 1964.

39766

GENERAL DYNAMICS F-111A

General Dynamics F-111A, 66-0036, 389th Tactical Fighter Squadron, 366th Tactical Fighter Wing, Mountain Home Air Force Base, 1982. The 389th TFS was responsible for training F-111 aircrews from 1979 to 1991.

GENERAL DYNAMICS F-111A

General Dynamics F-111A, 67-113, 430th Tactical Fighter Squadron, 474th Tactical Fighter Wing, Nellis Air Force Base, Nevada, 1977. This F-111 is shown with its weapons bay open.

Mach 1.3 two months later. Unofficially, it was nicknamed 'Aardvark'. The first F-111B flew on May 18, 1965. Later F-111As and all Bs had TF30-P-3 engines and a top speed of Mach 2.3.

After a protracted period of testing and alterations to the engine intake design during 1965 and 1966, the first example was delivered to the USAF on July 17, 1967. A modified version with more powerful engines, better intakes, digital avionics and a glass cockpit was ordered as the F-111D in 1967 and when this was delayed a simplified version was built as the F-111E with the original engine and avionics.

The F-111A became active with the 428th Tactical Fighter Squadron on April 28, 1968. Six aircraft were sent to Vietnam for testing in real combat conditions but three aircraft were lost in a month due to tailplane malfunction. Later that year, cracks in the wing attachment points were detected during fatigue testing and the F-111A fleet was grounded. The F-111B was cancelled in July 1968 and just seven had been completed by February 1969.

Another USAF variant, the F-111F, was ordered in 1969. This had the powerful TF30-P-100 engine and strengthened wings. Production commenced in 1970 just as deliveries of the F-111D were beginning. The F-111D did not enter operational service until 1972 due to problems with its cutting-edge digital

avionics and even then only equipped the 27th Tactical Fighter Wing at Cannon Air Force Base in New Mexico. The F-111A recommenced combat operations in Southeast Asia in September 1972.

A total of 158 F-111As were made including 17 pre-production aircraft being upgraded to production standard. Between March 1977 and November 1981, a total of 42 F-111As were converted into EF-111A Ravens as electronic warfare aircraft. All surviving unmodified F-111As were mothballed in 1991. There were 96 F-111Ds and these were withdrawn from service at around the same time.

The last of 94 F-111Es were retired in 1995, with the last of 106 F-111Fs being withdrawn the following year. Surviving EF-111As were mothballed in May 1998.●

GENERAL DYNAMICS F-111A

General Dynamics F-111A, 66-018, 428th Tactical Fighter Squadron, Takhli Royal Thai Air Base, Thailand, 1968. The Aardvark saw action for the first time in Vietnam during Operation Combat Lancer, from March to November of 1968.

McDONNELL DOUGLAS F-15 EAGLE

Designed as a pure air-superiority fighter in the 1970s, the superb F-15 has proven to be just as capable in the interdiction and ground-attack roles. Still in service today, it remains an incredibly versatile and effective aircraft.

1972–PRESENT

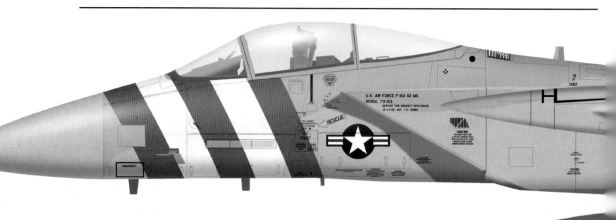

McDONNELL DOUGLAS F-15B-7-MC EAGLE

McDonnell Douglas F-15B-7-MC Eagle, 73-0108, 555th Tactical Fighter Training Squadron, Luke Air Force Base, Arizona, 1974. TAC-1 was the first operational F-15B and was used to train the initial cadre of F-15 crews.

During early 1965 it was decided that a new fighter was needed for the USAF which could effectively counter growing Soviet air-to-air capability. It was clear that the F-111A lacked the necessary manoeuvrability to combat enemy fighters and was too expensive to build in large numbers. A low-cost 'tactical fighter' that could be built in numbers to supplement the relatively small F-111A fleet was needed.

Existing designs were studied and both the Northrop F-5 Freedom Fighter and Vought A-7 Corsair II were considered. The A-7 won but there was growing support for a new more expensive fighter with greater air-to-air abilities – the F-X. A request for proposals was sent out to 13 companies on December 8, 1965, and eight companies responded. This was narrowed down to just four companies and between them,

up to July 1966, they came up with around 500 design concepts.

These typically had advanced aerodynamic features such as variable-sweep wings, weighed around 60,000lb and had a top speed of about Mach 2.7 – making them not dissimilar to the F-111 TFX.

In combat over Vietnam, American aircraft designed for high speed and long-range combat using missiles had found themselves at a disadvantage during close range encounters with slower but more manoeuvrable opponents equipped with built-in cannon. Within the USAF a small advocacy group had been formed comprising Colonel Everest Riccioni, Pierre Sprey and Colonel John Boyd who believed that the F-X programme was heading in the wrong direction. They argued that a lighter, slower, cheaper but much more manoeuvrable

fighter was needed. This could be built in large numbers to ensure air superiority.

Boyd had been assigned to review the F-X studies in October 1966 and along with civilian analyst Sprey put forward a case for a lighter F-X. A revised set of specifications, including a maximum take-off weight of 40,000lb, was issued in September 1968 and four companies submitted designs. General Dynamics was eliminated and McDonnell Douglas, Fairchild Republic and North American Rockwell went forward to the next stage in December 1968.

Each company had submitted its technical proposals by June 1969 and after extensive scrutiny McDonnell Douglas was announced as the ▶

McDONNELL DOUGLAS F-15A-9-MC EAGLE

McDonnell Douglas F-15A-9-MC Eagle, 73-0103, 461st Tactical Fighter Training Squadron, Luke Air Force Base, Arizona, 1975. This was one of the first operational F-15As.

McDonnell Douglas F-15 Eagle

McDONNELL DOUGLAS F-15A-17-MC EAGLE ▲

McDonnell Douglas F-15A-17-MC Eagle, 76-0111, 318th Fighter-Interceptor Squadron, McChord Air Force Base, Washington, 1984. The 318th FIS was tasked with the air defence of the Pacific Northwest and operated the F-15 from 1983 to 1989.

winner on December 23, 1969 – its characteristic flat broad fuselage, fixed wings, twin-fins, twin-engines and big intake design being based on one studied by NASA during wind tunnel tests. The engines were Pratt & Whitney F100s and an M61 Vulcan 20mm cannon was fitted as standard. The F-15 had two hardpoints under its wings, each able to take a pair of missile launch rails, four hardpoints on the underside

of its fuselage for semi-recessed AIM-7 Sparrows and a centreline pylon. Optional fuselage pylons could also be fitted.

Initially, it was equipped with the Hughes AN/APG-63 'look-down-shoot-down' radar. This advanced unit meant that the single-seat F-15A did not require a back-seater for radar management and was a significant technological leap forward from the radar systems employed by the F-4. It had almost four and a half

times the search volume and almost double the search range at 80NM.

The F-15A also employed a Head-Up Display to replace the traditional gunsight – the first time this revolutionary system had been employed in a pure fighter. Another innovation was Hands On Throttle And Stick or 'HOTAS', a system where the aircraft's most important controls are integrated into the pilot's joystick and throttle control. Using these ▶

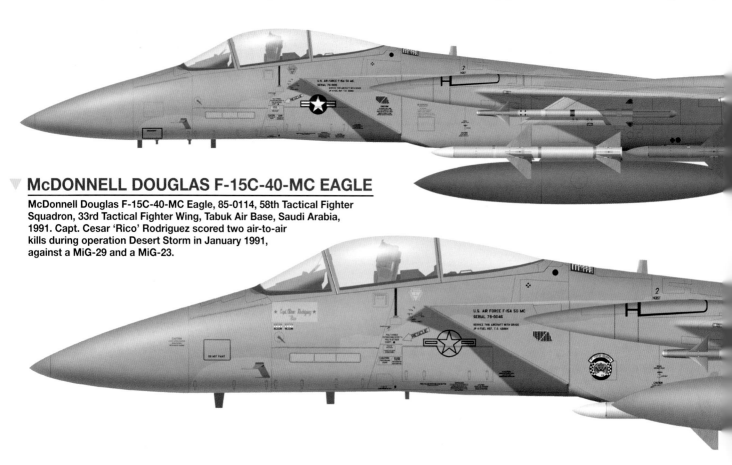

▼ McDONNELL DOUGLAS F-15C-40-MC EAGLE

McDonnell Douglas F-15C-40-MC Eagle, 85-0114, 58th Tactical Fighter Squadron, 33rd Tactical Fighter Wing, Tabuk Air Base, Saudi Arabia, 1991. Capt. Cesar 'Rico' Rodriguez scored two air-to-air kills during operation Desert Storm in January 1991, against a MiG-29 and a MiG-23.

McDONNELL DOUGLAS F-15A-15-MC EAGLE

McDonnell Douglas F-15A-15-MC Eagle, 76-0015, 5th Fighter-Interceptor Squadron, Minot Air
Force Base, North Dakota, 1986. The 5th FIS's F-106s were replaced with Eagles, which were
operated from 1984 to 1988.

McDONNELL DOUGLAS F-15C-25-MC EAGLE

McDonnell Douglas F-15C-25-MC Eagle, 79-0047, 525th Tactical Fighter
Squadron, 36th Tactical Fighter Wing, Bitburg Air Base, West Germany, 1987.
F-15s from the 525th stationed in West Germany constituted the first line of air
defence against a possible Warsaw pact invasion.

two systems in tandem, the F-15's pilot would have no need to take his eyes off the fight while hunting around for an elusive button or switch within the cockpit.

Two variants of the newly designated F-15 were ordered: the single seat F-15A and the two-seater F-15B (originally designated TF-15A). The first completed prototype, serial number 71-0280, was rolled out on June 26, 1972, and the type's new name – Eagle – along with the aircraft itself were revealed to the world for the first time. The aircraft was then dismantled and

loaded into the hold of a Lockheed C-5A Galaxy before being flown to Edwards Air Force Base in California to begin its flight testing regime.

At 7am on July 27, 1972, the reassembled aircraft flew under its own power for the first time. Despite concerns about one of the undercarriage doors failing to close correctly, the flight was a great success. Further testing followed but surprisingly few faults were found with the design. The tailplanes and wings received slight modifications to cure buffeting problems.

McDONNELL DOUGLAS F-15C-38-MC EAGLE ▽

McDonnell Douglas F-15C-38-MC Eagle, 84-0025, 44th
Tactical Fighter Squadron, Kadena Air Base, Japan, 2008.
This aircraft displays two kill marks achieved during
operation Desert Storm.

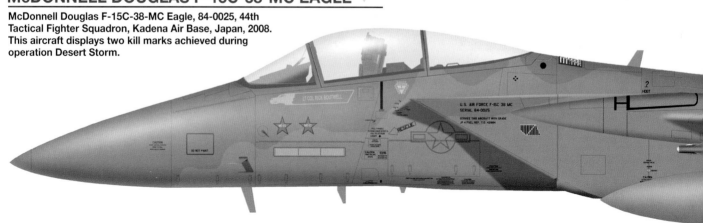

McDONNELL DOUGLAS F-15C-41-MC EAGLE ▽

McDonnell Douglas F-15C-41-MC Eagle, 86-0156, 493rd Tactical Fighter Squadron, 48th Tactical Fighter Wing, RAF Lakenheath, UK, 2017. Seen in 2017, this aircraft still displays the two kill marks achieved by Capt. Jeffrey Hwang against Serbian MiG-29s during Operation Allied Force in March 1999.

The last of 10 F-15A prototypes, serial 71-0289, made its flight debut on January 30, 1974. The first of two prototype F-15Bs, serial 71-0290, first flew on July 7, 1973, and the second, 71-0291, first flew on October 18, 1973.

The first F-15 to be delivered was an F-15B on November 13, 1974, and the first front line unit to receive one was the 555th Tactical Fighter Squadron. A total of 384 F-15As and 61 F-15Bs were manufactured between 1972 and 1979.

A new single seater all-weather air-superiority version, the F-15C, was introduced in 1979. Externally it differed little from the original F-15A but there were significant changes internally. The undercarriage was strengthened to cope with a greater maximum weight – up to 68,000lb – and the F-100 engines were improved. The airframe itself was also strengthened, allowing the pilot to pull 9 g, compared to the previous limit of 7.5 g.

The AN/APG-63 benefitted from greatly increased processing power and additional internal fuel tank capacity was provided. The aircraft could be fitted with fixed external conformal tanks for an even greater fuel load if required. There was also a new ejection seat known as the Advanced Concept Ejection Seat or 'ACES II' which improved pilot survivability in the event of an urgent departure being required.

A total of 483 F-15Cs were built along with 92 examples of the two-seater training version – the F-15D. The last 43 F-15Cs were upgraded to receive the AN/APG-70 radar and later the AN/APG-63(V)1 radar.

Although the F-15 was designed as an air superiority fighter, even as the first ▶

McDONNELL DOUGLAS F-15D-36-MC EAGLE ◢

McDonnell Douglas F-15D-36-MC Eagle, 83-050, United States Air Force Warfare Center, Nellis AFB, 2007. The USAF Warfare Center is responsible for advanced pilot training and testing and evaluation for the Air Force. It was renamed the USAFWC in 2005, having previously been the U.S. Air Force Tactical Fighter Weapons Center.

McDONNELL DOUGLAS F-15D-29-MC EAGLE ▽

McDonnell Douglas F-15D-29-MC Eagle, 80-058, 65th Aggressor Squadron, Nellis Air Force Base, Nevada, 2005. The 65th provided adversary aircraft for realistic air crews training – its F-15s were painted in colour schemes similar to those of Su-27 Flankers.

McDONNELL DOUGLAS ▷ F-15C-28-MC EAGLE

McDonnell Douglas F-15C-28-MC Eagle, 80-0038, 57th Fighter Squadron, Keflavik Airport, Iceland, 1995. Although all F-15C can carry FAST pack conformal fuel tanks, only a handful of USAF units regularly use it such as the Iceland-based 57th squadron.

prototypes were being tested McDonnell Douglas had given some thought to a ground-attack version – potentially as a future replacement for the F-111 and the company's own F-4. The firm's opportunity came when the USAF started the Tactical All-Weather Requirement Study in 1978. The F-15E, at this stage based on a modified F-15B, was submitted as a strike fighter while the USAF considered whether to buy more F-111Fs.

The study came out in favour of the F-15E and the following year McDonnell Douglas began working closely with Hughes on developing the F-15's ground-attack capabilities – although no contract had been placed for the type. The second two-seat TF-15A prototype, serial 71-0291, was modified to accommodate a Pave Tack laser

designator targeting pod allowing the delivery of guided bombs and made its first flight as the Advanced Fighter Capability Demonstrator on July 8, 1980.

The USAF launched the Enhanced Tactical Fighter programme in March 1981 with the goal of finding a direct replacement for the F-111. The requirement was for an aircraft capable of flying strike missions without the need for an additional fighter escort – it would effectively escort itself. The Panavia Tornado was considered for the role but the USAF considered that it lacked air-superiority credentials. General Dynamics put forward the F-16XL – a cranked arrow delta wing version of the F-16 and McDonnell Douglas submitted the F-15E.

The competition was renamed Dual-Role Fighter and evaluation of

proposals lasted until April 30, 1983. Both the General Dynamics and McDonnell Douglas designs were found to have real merit and McDonnell Douglas converted three more F-15s to join the evaluation process. The F-15E was finally declared the winner on February 24, 1984 – mainly because the aircraft embodied a significantly lower development cost of

McDONNELL DOUGLAS
F-15A-17-MC EAGLE

McDonnell Douglas F-15A-17-MC
Eagle, 76-0086, 6512th Test
Squadron, Edwards Air Force Base,
1985. This F-15, taking off from
Vandenberg AFB, was used to test
fire the Vought ASM-135 ASAT
antisatellite missile. The test, on
September 13, 1985, achieved a
direct hit on the targeted satellite.

$270 million compared to $470 million
for the F-16XL but also because it had
twin-engine redundancy compared to the
F-16XL's single engine configuration.

A figure of 400 aircraft was initially
discussed before a final total of 392 was
settled on. Work on building a trio of
F-15Es commenced in July 1985 and
the first flew on December 11, 1986. ▶

McDONNELL DOUGLAS
F-15E-41-MC STRIKE EAGLE

McDonnell Douglas F-15E-41-MC Strike Eagle, 86-0183,
Edwards Air Force Base, California, 1987. This was the
first production Strike Eagle and carried appropriated
titles on its nose.

McDonnell Douglas F-15 Eagle

McDONNELL DOUGLAS ▶
F-15E-52-MC STRIKE EAGLE

McDonnell Douglas F-15E-52-MC Strike
Eagle, 91-0322, 422nd Test & Evaluation
Squadron, 53rd Test & Evaluation Group,
Nellis Air Force Base, Nevada, 2019. Eagles
have a nuclear delivery capacity and tests
are being conduct on new freefall
tactical nuclear weapons such as the
B61-12 as depicted in this image.

The aircraft, serial 86-0183, had a
redesigned forward fuselage but carried
over the original F-15 rear fuselage
and engine bay. The second prototype
included the new rear fuselage and the
third incorporated all of the production
model F-15E's features.

The F-15E is powered by a pair of
Pratt & Whitney F100-PW-220 or -229
afterburning turbofans and is structurally
stronger than earlier F-15s. The weapons
systems officer position in the back
seat has multiple screens displaying
data from radar, electronic warfare
systems and thermographic cameras
plus an electronic map for navigation.
It also has a full set of dual controls so
that the WSO can take over flying the
aircraft if necessary.

The F-15E is fitted with fuselage-
hugging conformal fuel tanks as
standard and has an integrated tactical
electronic warfare system including
radar warning receivers, radar jammer,
radar and chaff/flare dispensers. An
external ALQ-131 ECM pod can be
added to the aircraft's centreline pylon
as required.

The McDonnell Douglas F-15
became the Boeing F-15 in 1997
following the merger of the two
companies, with the latter being the
'surviving' brand. In 2010, the F-15E
fleet was upgraded to carry the
Raytheon APG-82 Active Electronically
Scanned Array (AESA) radar. This

McDONNELL DOUGLAS F-15E-44-MC STRIKE EAGLE

McDonnell Douglas F-15E-44-MC Strike Eagle, 87-0207, 366th Fighter Squadron, 4th Fighter Wing, Seymour Johnson Air Force Base, 1991. This Strike Eagle displays mission markings on the nose after its participation in Operation Desert Storm.

combines the processor of the F/A-18E/F Super Hornet's APG-79 with the antenna of the APG-63(V)3 AESA from the F-15C.

The first F-15E was delivered to the 405th Tactical Training Wing in April 1988 and the type continued in production into 2001 with a total of 236 having been completed. The USAF stated in 2017 that it intended to continue flying its F-15C/D into the 2020s and the F-15E is expected to remain in service until at least 2025. At the time of writing no firm replacement had yet been decided upon. In April 2019 it was reported that the USAF may yet buy a new batch of fully modernised F-15s, having submitted a budget request for eight new F-15EXs in 2020 and 72 more over the next four years.

Famously undefeated in air-to-air combat with a kill ratio of more than 100-0, the F-15 continues to rank among the world's most powerful, versatile and deadly warplanes.●

BOEING F-15EX ▼

Boeing F-15EX, 2027. In 2019, the USAF confirmed plans to acquire the new F-15EX variant, featuring many capacities presented in late export models. This is a speculative representation of how one of those aircraft might appear.

GENERAL DYNA
F-16 FIGHTING

1974–PRESENT

The highly capable and thoroughly modern multirole F-16, commonly known as the Viper despite its 'official nickname', forms the backbone of the USAF's fighter force.

The F-X programme was launched in 1965 to procure a new fighter at a time when combat in Vietnam was reshaping the USAF's understanding of what a fighter needed to be. Up to that point it was considered that high-speed missile platforms with ever more powerful long-range radar systems were the future.

MICS FALCON

GENERAL DYNAMICS F-16A BLOCK 1

General Dynamics F-16A Block 1, 78-0016, 16th Tactical Fighter Training Squadron, Hill Air Force Base, Utah, 1979. The first F-16s were delivered to the 16th TFTS in 1979.

GENERAL DYNAMICS F-16B BLOCK 1

General Dynamics F-16B Block 1, 78-082, 16th Tactical Fighter Training Squadron, Hill AFB, 1979. The first F-16s were delivered with a black radome, but due to its high visibility this was changed to a more appropriate colour.

But the experience of pilots fighting MiGs in the teeth of sophisticated surface-to-air missile defences challenged this view and a new way of thinking began to permeate the decision-making process. Colonel John Boyd was among the first to champion the view that a lightweight fighter capable of extreme manoeuvres at low speed would provide superior air-to-air combat capability.

Together with Colonel Everest Riccioni and civilian analyst Pierre Sprey he formed what became known as the 'Fighter Mafia' to campaign for a lighter F-X. Many within the air force dismissed Boyd's views because they were perceived as a threat to what would become the F-15. But a key component of Boyd's pitch was cost – the lightweight fighter would be much cheaper and could therefore be bought in much larger numbers. This was a perspective likely to win friends within the USAF's highly budget-conscious upper echelons.

Rather than replacing the F-X, the lightweight fighter concept became ▶

General Dynamics F-16 Fighting Falcon

GENERAL DYNAMICS F-16B BLOCK 1 ▶

General Dynamics F-16B Block 1, 78-088, Air Force Flight Test Center,
Edwards Air Force base, California, 1990. This was one of the longest
serving F-16s – regularly flying from 1979 into the early 2000s.

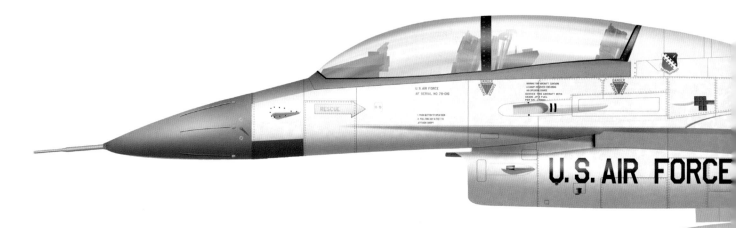

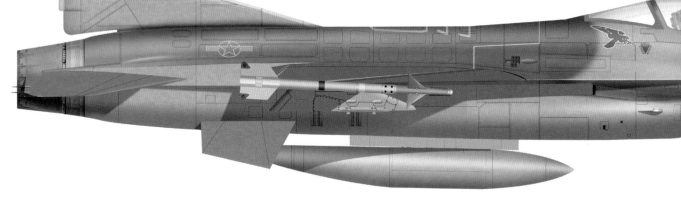

a competition in its own right: F-XX.
The Air Force Prototype Study Group
was formed in May 1971 and one of its
proposals was the Lightweight Fighter
(LWF). A request for proposals (RFP) was
drawn up which called for a 20,000lb
day fighter optimised for combat at
speeds of between Mach 0.6 and Mach
1.6 at altitudes of between 30,000ft

and 40,000ft. It had to have excellent
manoeuvrability, range and acceleration
and ideally the cost of a single unit
needed to be £3 million. The RFP was
subsequently issued on January 6, 1972.

Five companies offered designs and
these were quickly narrowed down
to Northrop's twin-engine P-600 and
General Dynamics' single engine Model

GENERAL DYNAMICS F-16A BLOCK 15 ▶

General Dynamics F-16A Block 15, 82-0938, 93rd Fighter Squadron,
Air Force Reserve, Homestead Air Force Base, 2005.

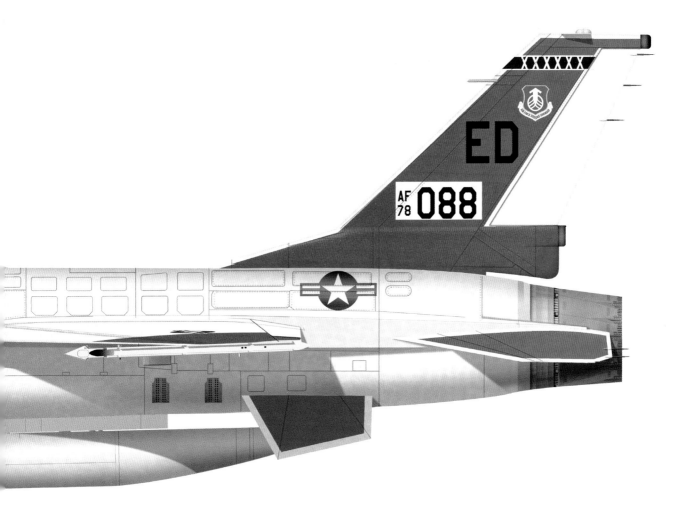

401. Each company received a contract and funding to build two prototypes of its design, these being designated YF-17 and YF-16 respectively. Although there remained opponents to the LWF, the fact that it would be so cheap won it plenty of supporters. The Fighter Mafia successfully argued that the LWF and the F-15 would form a 'high-cost/low-

cost mix' or 'high/low mix' for short.

The team designing the YF-16 was led by Harry Hillaker, who had also worked on the F-111, and the first prototype was rolled out on December 13, 1973. Its first official flight was made on February 2, 1974 – although it had previously become airborne for six minutes following a high-speed taxi test on January 20, 1974. The

second prototype first flew on May 9, 1974. Northrop's YF-17 prototypes first flew on June 9 and August 21.

The LWF competition soon became an acquisition programme with the advanced but inexpensive fighters attracting attention from other NATO air forces. With the F-15 filling the pure air-superiority role, the USAF badly needed ▶

GENERAL DYNAMICS F-16A BLOCK 15

General Dynamics F-16A Block 15, 82-0946, 613rd Tactical Fighter Squadron, Torrejon Air base, Spain, 1984.

a replacement for its F-4 and F-105 fighter-bombers and it was therefore decided that the LWF should have multirole capability and would be ordered alongside the F-15 – placating the LWF's remaining detractors.

The YF-16 proved to be more manoeuvrable than the YF-17 and also had the advantage of having the same engine as the F-15, ensuring parts commonality and lowering costs. As a result it was announced as the competition winner on January 13, 1975. Less than four months later, the US Navy ordered the YF-17 as the basis for the F/A-18 Hornet.

Although 15 'full-scale development' F-16s were initially ordered by the USAF for flight testing, this was soon cut back to just six F-16A single seaters and two F-16B two-seaters. The YF-16 fuselage was lengthened by 10.6in and a larger nose was added to accommodate the AN/APG-66 radar. Wing area was increased from 280sq ft to 300sq ft and the number of stores stations was increased by two. The tail surfaces were also enlarged.

The first 'development' F-16A was rolled out on October 20, 1976, and made its debut flight on December 8. The first development F-16B began flight testing on August 8, 1977, and the first full production model F-16A took its first flight on August 7, 1978. The latter was delivered to the USAF on January 6, 1979, and the type received its official nickname 'Fighting Falcon' on July 21, 1980. The first operational non-training unit to receive the F-16A, on October 1, 1980, was the 34th Tactical Fighter Squadron.

The following year, after concerns were raised about the aircraft's potential for deep stall at high angles of attack, 25% larger tailplanes were added to the F-16 design and retrofitted to earlier production models.

▼ GENERAL DYNAMICS F-16C BLOCK 25

General Dynamics F-16C Block 25, 85-479, 527th Tactical Fighter Squadron, RAF Woodbridge, UK, 1988. The 527th provided aggressor aircraft for realistic air combat training for USAFE forces.

GENERAL DYNAMICS F-16C BLOCK 40 ▲

General Dynamics F-16C Block 40, 90-0776, 74th Tactical Fighter
▶ Squadron, Pope Air Force Base, North Carolina, 1995.

THE FIRST 'DEVELOPMENT' F-16A WAS ROLLED OUT ON OCTOBER 20, 1976, AND MADE ITS DEBUT FLIGHT ON DECEMBER 8. THE FIRST DEVELOPMENT F-16B BEGAN FLIGHT TESTING ON AUGUST 8, 1977, AND THE FIRST FULL PRODUCTION MODEL F-16A TOOK ITS FIRST FLIGHT ON AUGUST 7, 1978.

GENERAL DYNAMICS F-16A

General Dynamics F-16A, 35th Tactical Fighter Squadron, Kunsan Air Base, South Korea, 1985.

GENERAL DYNAMICS F-16C BLOCK 25

General Dynamics F-16C Block 25, 83-1121, 312th Tactical Fighter Training Squadron, Luke Air Force Base, Arizona 1984. This was the first F-16C delivered to an operational unit.

General Dynamics F-16 Fighting Falcon

The single seat F-16C and its two-seat counterpart, the F-16D, were introduced in 1984 as Block 25 – with the first 'C' making its flying debut on June 19, 1984, and the type entering full production that December. These were powered by the Pratt & Whitney F100-PW-220E and featured improved avionics and radar, specifically the AN/APG-68, which allowed the use of beyond-visual-range AIM-7 and AIM-120 missiles. They also had improved ground-attack capability, being able to use the AIM-65D Maverick.

The next major update of the design came in 1986 with the F-16C/D Block 30/32. The biggest change was the switch to a new powerplant – the General Electric F110-GE-100 – for Block 30, with the Block 32 aircraft keeping the F100-PW-220E. The Block 30/32 aircraft could carry AGM-88A High-speed Anti-Radiation Missiles (HARMs) as well as the AGM-45 Shrike Anti-Radiation Missile (ARM). Avionics and decoy measures were also improved with twice the previous number of chaff/flare dispensers. The first example flew on June 12, 1986.

Block 40/42 was introduced in 1988. These have digital flight controls, replacing the old analogue system of the Block 25s, 30s and 32s. They also have an advanced holographic Head Up Display linked to a Martin Marietta LANTIRN (Low Altitude Navigation and Targeting Infra-Red, Night) targeting pod. Fitting this pod meant that the F-16's undercarriage legs actually had to be extended slightly for better ground clearance and the landing gear needed bigger wheels and tyres. The knock-on effect of this was a need for 'bulged' landing gear doors. This in turn meant that the aircraft's landing lights, which had been on the gear doors, had to be moved to the nose gear door.

GENERAL DYNAMICS F-16C BLOCK 25 ▼

General Dynamics F-16C Block 25, 83-1161, 33rd Tactical Fighter Squadron, Al Dhafra Air Base, UAE, 1991. F-16s made a significant contribution to both Operation Desert Shield and Desert Storm, performing many different roles in theatre.

An avionics upgrade means that Block 40/42 aircraft now have automatic terrain following and a new GPS navigation system plus new decoy launchers. The airframe itself was strengthened too, in order to cope with the additional weight of equipment. Block 40/42 F-16Cs and Ds can now use the Paveway family of guided weapons including the GBU-10, GBU-12 and GBU-24 Paveway laser-guided bombs and the GBU-15 glide bomb.

Pilots flying Block 40/42 F-16s are able to use night vision goggles and there is a data-link system which allows

Forward Air Controllers to upload new data directly to the aircraft's weapons system computer which then puts it onto the pilot's HUD. Block 40/42 aircraft were also part of the Have Glass programme, intended to reduce their radar signature. This features a gold-tinted 'indium tin oxide' cockpit canopy and radar absorbent material including paint, making the aircraft up to 15% more difficult to detect.

The newest version of the F-16 currently in use by the USAF is the Block 50/52 – designed to complement the Block 40/42. This version features the

Honeywell H-423 Ring Laser Gyro Inertial Navigation System (RLG INS), enabling quicker in-flight alignment, an enhanced GPS receiver, AN/ALR-56M advanced radar warning receivers and a Tracor ▶

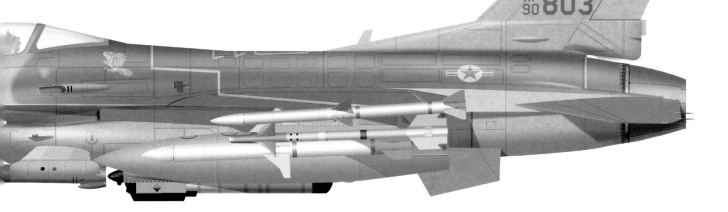

GENERAL DYNAMICS F-16C (J) BLOCK 50

General Dynamics F-16C (J) Block 50, 90-0803, 14th Tactical Fighter Squadron, Misawa Air Base, Japan, 2007. F-16CJ is the unofficial designation of these aircraft – which have a Wild Weasel role.

GENERAL DYNAMICS F-16C

General Dynamics F-16C, 85-0416, 313th Tactical Fighter Squadron, Hahn Air Base, West Germany, 1988. USAF F-16s have a tactical nuclear delivery capability; this aircraft is armed with a B61 training bomb.

General Dynamics F-16 Fighting Falcon

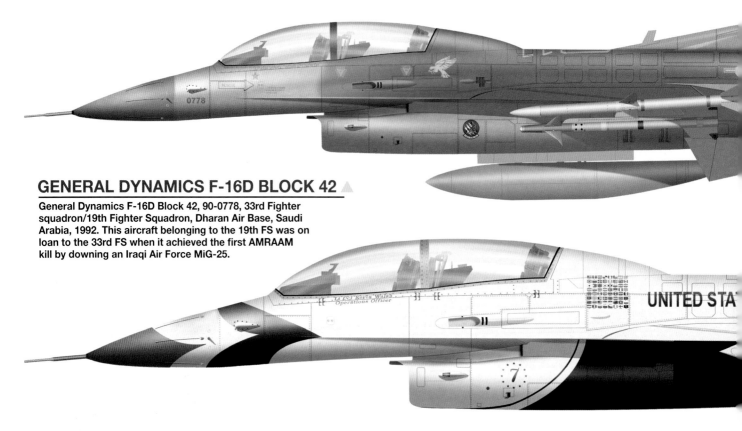

GENERAL DYNAMICS F-16D BLOCK 42 ▲

General Dynamics F-16D Block 42, 90-0778, 33rd Fighter squadron/19th Fighter Squadron, Dharan Air Base, Saudi Arabia, 1992. This aircraft belonging to the 19th FS was on loan to the 33rd FS when it achieved the first AMRAAM kill by downing an Iraqi Air Force MiG-25.

GENERAL DYNAMICS F-16D BLOCK 52 ▲

General Dynamics F-16D Block 52, 91-0479, number 7, Thunderbirds, 2016. F-16s are the current aircraft operated by the Thunderbirds display team.

GENERAL DYNAMICS ▽
F-16C BLOCK 42

General Dynamics F-16C Block 42, 88-548, 64th Aggressor Squadron, Nellis Air Force Base, Nevada, 2007.

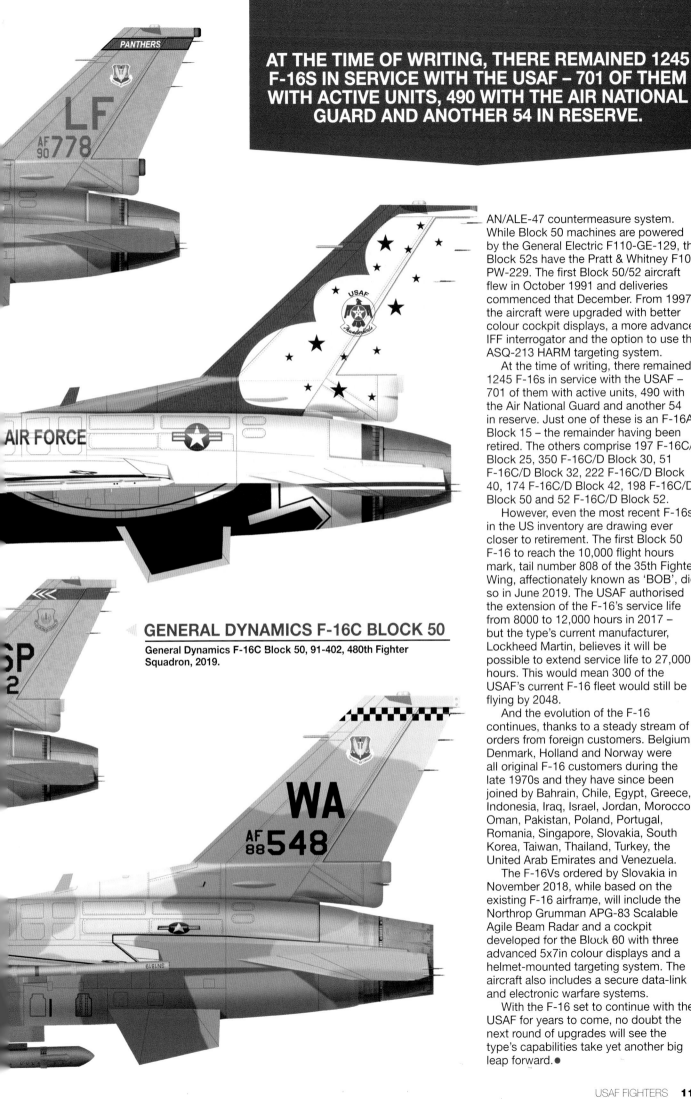

GENERAL DYNAMICS F-16C BLOCK 50

General Dynamics F-16C Block 50, 91-402, 480th Fighter Squadron, 2019.

AN/ALE-47 countermeasure system. While Block 50 machines are powered by the General Electric F110-GE-129, the Block 52s have the Pratt & Whitney F100-PW-229. The first Block 50/52 aircraft flew in October 1991 and deliveries commenced that December. From 1997, the aircraft were upgraded with better colour cockpit displays, a more advanced IFF interrogator and the option to use the ASQ-213 HARM targeting system.

At the time of writing, there remained 1245 F-16s in service with the USAF – 701 of them with active units, 490 with the Air National Guard and another 54 in reserve. Just one of these is an F-16A Block 15 – the remainder having been retired. The others comprise 197 F-16C/D Block 25, 350 F-16C/D Block 30, 51 F-16C/D Block 32, 222 F-16C/D Block 40, 174 F-16C/D Block 42, 198 F-16C/D Block 50 and 52 F-16C/D Block 52.

However, even the most recent F-16s in the US inventory are drawing ever closer to retirement. The first Block 50 F-16 to reach the 10,000 flight hours mark, tail number 808 of the 35th Fighter Wing, affectionately known as 'BOB', did so in June 2019. The USAF authorised the extension of the F-16's service life from 8000 to 12,000 hours in 2017 – but the type's current manufacturer, Lockheed Martin, believes it will be possible to extend service life to 27,000 hours. This would mean 300 of the USAF's current F-16 fleet would still be flying by 2048.

And the evolution of the F-16 continues, thanks to a steady stream of orders from foreign customers. Belgium, Denmark, Holland and Norway were all original F-16 customers during the late 1970s and they have since been joined by Bahrain, Chile, Egypt, Greece, Indonesia, Iraq, Israel, Jordan, Morocco, Oman, Pakistan, Poland, Portugal, Romania, Singapore, Slovakia, South Korea, Taiwan, Thailand, Turkey, the United Arab Emirates and Venezuela.

The F-16Vs ordered by Slovakia in November 2018, while based on the existing F-16 airframe, will include the Northrop Grumman APG-83 Scalable Agile Beam Radar and a cockpit developed for the Block 60 with three advanced 5x7in colour displays and a helmet-mounted targeting system. The aircraft also includes a secure data-link and electronic warfare systems.

With the F-16 set to continue with the USAF for years to come, no doubt the next round of upgrades will see the type's capabilities take yet another big leap forward.●

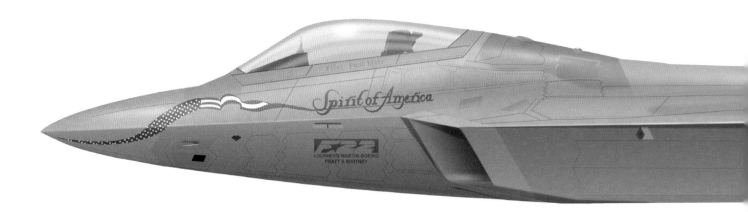

LOCKHEED MARTIN F-22 RAPTOR

The state-of-the-art F-22 is the original fifth generation stealth fighter and shows no signs of being surpassed by its more recent rivals.

1997–PRESENT

LOCKHEED-MARTIN F-22A-1-LM RAPTOR

Lockheed-Martin F-22A-1-LM Raptor, 91-4001, 1997. Spirit of America and Raptor One were the slogans displayed on the first engineering, manufacturing and development EMD F-22A when it was presented.

W ith the F-15 and F-16 entering service, the USAF set about making plans for their replacement. Technology was advancing at a rapid pace with new lightweight alloys, composite materials, powerful propulsion systems and stealth technology reaching the point of viability for a full production model aircraft for the first time.

The Advanced Tactical Fighter programme was launched in 1981 and after four years of assessment, consultation and consideration a request for proposals was issued in September 1985. This emphasised the need to employ both stealth and supercruise technology. Seven companies put forward designs – Lockheed, Boeing, General Dynamics, McDonnell Douglas, Northrop, Grumman and Rockwell – and these were narrowed down to the proposals of Lockheed and Northrop on October 31, 1986. But rather than the unsuccessful companies simply being knocked out of contention, Boeing and General Dynamics formed a partnership

with Lockheed while McDonnell Douglas joined the Northrop bid.

The two teams of contractors then commenced design, research, development and prototype construction – a process known as demonstration and validation or 'Dem/Val' which lasted for four years and two months. Each built two prototypes of its design, one for each of the engine options available – the Pratt & Whitney YF119 and the General Electric YF120.

Northrop's first YF-23 made its first flight on August 27, 1990, while Lockheed's first YF-22 made its flight debut on September 29, 1990. Comparative testing indicated that the YF-23 was faster and stealthier while the YF-22 had the edge when it came to manoeuvrability. Both teams submitted the results of their evaluations

in December 1990 and the YF-22 was announced as the winner on April 23, 1991, with the YF119 being selected as the winning engine for the F-22 production model.

The F-22A differed significantly from the YF-22 in having a leading edge wing sweepback of 42 compared to 48 and its fins were repositioned further towards the rear of the aircraft while being reduced in surface area by 20%. The cockpit canopy was moved closer to the nose by 7in to improve pilot visibility and the engine intakes were moved 14in further to the rear. The trailing edges of the wings and tailplanes were altered as work progressed to improve their strength and stealth characteristics.

The F-22A's two closely spaced Pratt & Whitney F119-PW-100 augmented turbofan engines have pitch-axis thrust ▶

LOCKHEED-MARTIN F-22A-35-LM RAPTOR

Lockheed-Martin F-22A-35-LM Raptor, 09-4176, 27th Fighter Squadron. The 27th was the first Raptor combat squadron.

LOCKHEED-MARTIN F-22A-30-LM RAPTOR ▷

Lockheed-Martin F-22A-30-LM Raptor, 05-4106, 7th Fighter Squadron, Holloman Air Force Base, New Mexico, 2008. The Raptor has a ventral and two lateral weapons bays seen here in their open positions.

vectoring nozzles with a movement range of plus or minus 20. Each provides 35,000lb-ft of thrust, giving a top speed of Mach 1.8 when flying in fuel-conserving supercruise mode – without afterburners – and above Mach 2 with afterburning.

Avionics include the Sanders/ General Electric AN/ALR-94 electronic warfare system, Lockheed Martin AN/ AAR-56 infra-red and ultraviolet missile launch detector and a Westinghouse/ Texas Instruments AN/APG-77 active electronically scanned array radar. The AN/ARL-94 is a passive radar detector with more than 30 antennas blended into the wings and fuselage to provide all-round radar warning receiver coverage. Its range exceeds that of the aircraft's own radar. The APG-77 itself can track multiple targets under any weather conditions and the data it provides, along with data from the aircraft's other sensors, is processed by a pair of Hughes Common Integrated Processors, each able to process up to 10.5 billion instructions per second. The data is then presented to the pilot as a combined view. The F-22 can also function as a mini-AWACS thanks to its aircraft threat detection and identification capability and can quickly designate targets for allies and coordinate friendly aircraft.

LOCKHEED-MARTIN F-22A-10-LM RAPTOR ▽

Lockheed-Martin F-22A-10-LM Raptor, 99-4011, 433rd Weapons Squadron, 57th Wing, Nellis Air Force Base, Nevada. Part of the USAF Weapons School, the 433rd WS provides Weapons Instructors courses.

LOCKHEED-MARTIN F-22A-10-LM RAPTOR

Lockheed-Martin F-22A-10-LM Raptor, 00-4013, 43rd Fighter Squadron, 325th Fighter Wing, Tyndall Air Force Base, Florida. The 43rd FS remains the Formal Training Unit for the type.

Inside the F-22A's cockpit is an array of all-digital flight instruments. The HUD is the primary flight instrument but information is also supplied to the pilot via six liquid-crystal colour display panels.

The aircraft carries all of its stores internally, with a single large payload bay on the underside of the fuselage and two smaller bays on the sides of the fuselage. In these it can carry a wide variety of munitions, from JDAM bombs to AIM-120

AMRAAM missiles. The F-22 also has an internally mounted M61A2 Vulcan 20mm cannon in its right wing root. The muzzle cover has a retractable door so that the aircraft's stealth profile can be maintained when it is not in use.

▶

Lockheed Martin F-22 Raptor

The aircraft's remarkable stealth capability comes from its airframe shape and its use of radar-absorbent materials – not to mention an attention to detail that has seen any hinges or other protrusions eliminated. A special paint reduces the F-22's infra-red signature and active cooling of its wing leading edges prevents a build-up of heat during supersonic flight.

A two-seater F-22B was originally planned but was cancelled in 1996. A medium-range FB-22 supersonic stealth bomber version was also proposed but this too was cancelled.

The first engineering and manufacturing development F-22 was rolled out on April 9, 1997, and made its first flight on September 7, 1997. From here, production would continue for 15 years. The USAF originally planned to order 750 F-22s for a total of $44.3 billion but the 1990 Major Aircraft Review saw this total reduced to 648 from 1996. The following year, the number fell to 339 and in 2003 it dropped again to 277. A year later the Department of Defense slashed the programme still further to just 183 operational aircraft.

The cost of the F-22 programme continued to

rise throughout the 2000s and serious questions were asked about whether the aircraft was needed at all in the wake of the Cold War. In September 2006, Congress upheld a total ban on the sale of F-22s overseas in order to protect the aircraft's stealth technology and systems – although there was some thought given to lifting the ban in 2010. The total number of operational aircraft was set at 187 and the 195th and last example was completed in December

2011 before being delivered to the USAF on May 2, 2012.

As it became evident that next generation Russian and Chinese fifth generation aircraft were catching up with the latest American types, the House Armed Services Committee Tactical Air and Land Forces Subcommittee put forward legislation in April 2016 that would require the USAF to assess the costs likely to arise from resuming F-22 production. However, on June 9, 2017,

LOCKHEED-MARTIN F-22A-10-LM RAPTOR

Lockheed-Martin F-22A-10-LM Raptor, 91-4008, 411th Flight Test Squadron, Air Force Materiel Command 412th Test Wing, Edwards Air Force Base, California. This unit was responsible for the Advanced Tactical Fighter programme fly-off competition between the YF-22 and the YF-23 prototypes. After that the 411th FTS still performed tests on the F-22A Raptor.

THE F-22 COMBINES UNASSAILABLE AIR-SUPERIORITY PERFORMANCE WITH AN UNMATCHED STEALTH CAPABILITY, MAKING IT THE BEST FIGHTER YET BUILT ANYWHERE IN THE WORLD – THOUGH ITS ABILITIES ARE REFLECTED IN ITS PRICE TAG.

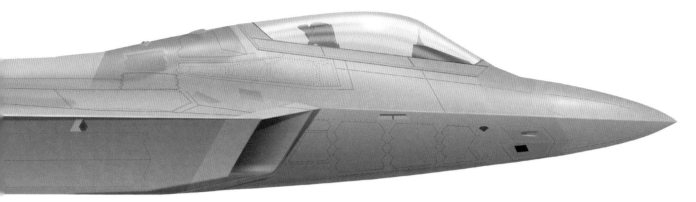

the USAF reported to Congress that there were no plans to restart F-22 production because the cost would be too great – about $50 billion for 194 aircraft, with each one costing between $206 million and $216 million plus one-off start-up costs.

The F-22 combines unassailable air-superiority performance with an unmatched stealth capability, making it the best fighter yet built anywhere in the world – though its abilities are reflected in its price tag.●

LOCKHEED-MARTIN F-22A-35-LM RAPTOR

Lockheed-Martin F-22A-35-LM Raptor, 09-4190, 90th Fighter Squadron, Pacific Air Forces 3rd Wing, Elmendorf Air Force Base, Alaska. Raptors can be equiped with external fuel tanks for ferry flights.

LOCKHEED-MARTIN F-22A RAPTOR

Lockheed-Martin F-22A Raptor, 1st Operations Group, 2019. During Operation Inherent Resolve, F-22s were deployed to the Middle East area and performed several missions such as ground strikes and ISR.

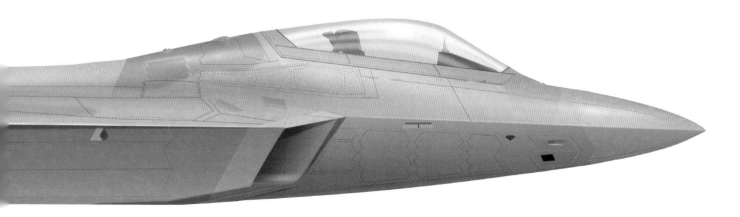

LOCKHEED-MARTIN F-35 LIGHTNING ▽

Lockheed-Martin F-35 Lightning, AF-01, 461st Flight Test Squadron, Edwards Air Force Base, California 2006. This aircraft was the first to be used for external weapons flight tests.

LOCKHEED MARTIN F-35 LIGHTNING II

2006-PRESENT

A fighter designed to be all things to all men might seem like a recipe for disaster but the F-35 – now entering active service with USAF units – embodies the very latest technology on all fronts and is undeniably the world's most advanced combat aircraft.

T he Joint Strike Fighter programme which would produce the F-35 was the result of two earlier programmes merging – Common Affordable Lightweight Fighter, intended to produce a VSTOL aircraft for the US Marine Corps and the British Royal Navy, and Joint Advanced Strike Technology (JAST).

The purpose of JAST was to develop an aircraft using the very latest technology

LOCKHEED-MARTIN F-35 LIGHTNING

Lockheed-Martin F-35 Lightning, AA-1, 461st Flight Test
Squadron, Edwards Air Force Base, California 2006. The first
F-35A was flown on December 15, 2006.

which could replace most US fighters with a single common design. Merging the two programmes meant that the new fighter would replace most US naval fighters too.

JAST studies led the Pentagon to continue with the F-22 for the USAF and F/A-18E/F Super Hornet for the US Navy but cancel two further programmes – Multi-Role Fighter and A/F-X. Procurement of the F-16 and F/A-18C/D was also reduced in anticipation of both types' ultimate replacement by the new common fighter.

Design studies from manufacturers McDonnell Douglas, Northrop Grumman, Lockheed Martin and Boeing were submitted for JAST in 1993 and the Joint Strike Fighter programme was launched in 1994. The goal was to create an affordable strike aircraft that would also be second only to the F-22 in the air supremacy role. In order to meet the requirements of such a diverse range of services and roles it would need to be available in three forms – one that took off and landed conventionally, one capable of short take off and vertical landing and a CATOBAR (carrier-based catapult assisted take-off but arrested recovery) version. In November 1995 the UK agreed to pay $200 million to buy in as a partner on the project.

A year later, on November 16, 1996, both Lockheed Martin and Boeing received $750 million contracts to develop prototypes. Lockheed Martin's design was given the designation X-35 and Boeing's X-32. Two X-35 prototypes were developed – the X-35A, later converted into the X-35B, and the X-35C, which had larger wings. The X-35A completed its first flight on October 24, 2000, and the process of converting it into the X-35B commenced on November 22, 2000. The X-35C made its first flight on December 16, 2000. During final qualifying Joint Strike Fighter flight trials, the X-35B STOVL (short take-off, vertical landing) aircraft was able to take off in less than 500ft, go supersonic, then land vertically – which Boeing's equivalent design was unable to match.

Lockheed Martin was declared the winner and awarded a contract for system development and demonstration on October 26, 2001. The JSF programme was by now being jointly funded by the US, UK, Italy, Holland, Canada, Turkey, Australia, Norway and Denmark.

During further development, Lockheed Martin slightly enlarged the X-35, stretching the forward fuselage by 5in to make additional space available

for the avionics. The tailplanes were correspondingly moved 2in further back to retain balance. The upper fuselage was raised by an inch along the centre line too. Parts manufacture for the first prototype began on November 10, 2003.

The X-35 had lacked a weapons bay and adding one resulted in design changes which increased the aircraft's weight by 2200lb. Lockheed Martin addressed this by increasing engine power, thinning the airframe members, reducing the size of the weapons bay itself and the size of the aircraft's fins. The electrical system also underwent changes, as did the section of the aircraft immediately behind the cockpit. All this succeeded in reducing weight by 2700lb but at a cost of $6.2 billion and 18 months of additional development time.

The F-35 is powered by a single 50,000lb thrust Pratt & Whitney F135 engine which, while it lacks a supercruise function, does enable the aircraft to fly at Mach 1.2 for 150 miles without using its afterburner. With afterburner, the F-35 has a top speed of Mach 1.6. The short take-off and vertical landing variant, the F-35B, has the Rolls-Royce LiftSystem. This features a thrust vectoring nozzle, allowing the

Lockheed Martin F-35 Lightning II

LOCKHEED MARTIN F-35A LIGHTNING ▲

Lockheed Martin F-35A Lightning, 07-0744, AF-06, 461st Flight Test Squadron, Edwards AFB, California 2011. The first production aircraft was delivered to the USAF in May 2011.

LOCKHEED MARTIN F-35A LIGHTNING ▲

Lockheed Martin F-35A Lightning, 14-5094, 34th Fighter Squadron, Hill Air Force Base, Utah, 2016. Equipped with the F-35A in 2015, the 34th Fighter Squadron was declared the first USAF squadron to achieve initial operational capability on the type the following year.

main engine exhaust to be deflected downward from the tail end of the aircraft.

Base armament is a GAU-22/A 25mm cannon mounted internally and carrying 182 rounds in the F-35A or externally as a pod with 220 rounds for the F-35B and C. The pod itself has stealth features. All three F-35 variants have four underwing pylons capable of carrying AIM-120 AMRAAMs, AGM-158 cruise missiles and guided bombs. They also have two near-wingtip pylons designed for the AIM-9X sidewinder and AIM-132 ASRAAM.

The F-35's two internal weapons bays can carry up to four weapons – two of them air-to-surface missiles or bombs and the other two air-to-air missiles such as the AIM-120 or AIM-132. Using both internal and external stations an air-to-air missile load of eight AIM-120s and two AIM-9s is possible.

Inside its cockpit, the F-35 has a 20x8in touchscreen, a speech-recognition system, a helmet-mounted display, a right-hand side stick controller, a Martin-Baker ejection seat and an oxygen generation system derived from that of the F-22. Due to the helmet display, the aircraft does not have a HUD.

Its radar is the AN/APG-81 developed by Northrop Grumman Electronic Systems with the addition of the nose-mounted Electro-Optical Targeting System. The F-35's electronic warfare suite is the AN/ASQ-239 (Barracuda) with sensor fusion of radio frequency and infrared tracking, advanced radar warning receiver including geolocation of targeting of threats, and multispectral image countermeasures.

The aircraft has 10 radio frequency antennas embedded in its wings and tail. Six passive infrared sensors are distributed across the F-35 as part of Northrop Grumman's AN/AAQ-37 distributed aperture system. This provides missile warning, reports missile launch locations, detects and tracks approaching aircraft and replaces traditional night vision devices.

The first F-35, AA-1, was rolled out

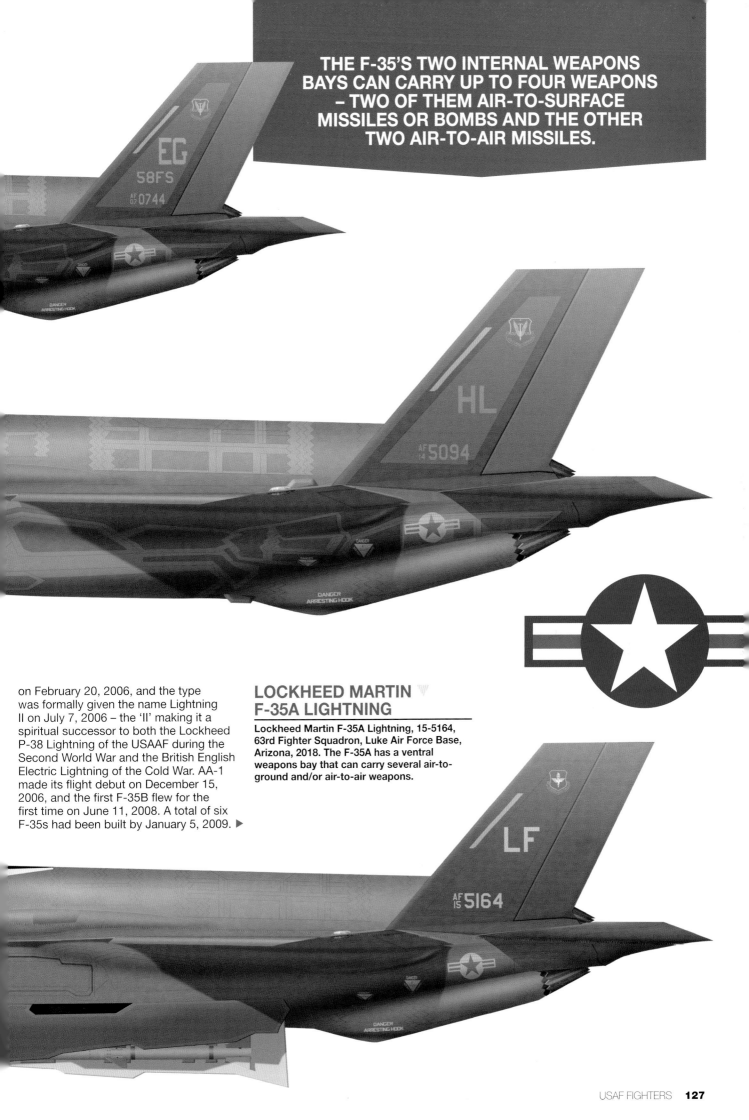

THE F-35'S TWO INTERNAL WEAPONS BAYS CAN CARRY UP TO FOUR WEAPONS – TWO OF THEM AIR-TO-SURFACE MISSILES OR BOMBS AND THE OTHER TWO AIR-TO-AIR MISSILES.

on February 20, 2006, and the type was formally given the name Lightning II on July 7, 2006 – the 'II' making it a spiritual successor to both the Lockheed P-38 Lightning of the USAAF during the Second World War and the British English Electric Lightning of the Cold War. AA-1 made its flight debut on December 15, 2006, and the first F-35B flew for the first time on June 11, 2008. A total of six F-35s had been built by January 5, 2009. ▶

LOCKHEED MARTIN
F-35A LIGHTNING

Lockheed Martin F-35A Lightning, 15-5164, 63rd Fighter Squadron, Luke Air Force Base, Arizona, 2018. The F-35A has a ventral weapons bay that can carry several air-to-ground and/or air-to-air weapons.

Lockheed Martin F-35 Lightning II

The F-35C made its flight debut on June 6, 2010, and the first production F-35A, known as AF-6, flew for the first time on February 25, 2011. The USAF formally accepted its first F-35A on May 5, 2011, and Lockheed Martin delivered the first F-35A to Eglin Air Force Base, Florida, on July 14, 2011 – ready for pilot and engineer training. The first F-35B was delivered to the US Marine Corps on July 11, 2012, and the UK formally received its first F-35B on July 12, 2012. The US Navy received its first F-35C on June 22, 2013.

The F-35 programme has proven highly controversial over the years – with cost overruns, delays and accusations of industrial espionage. The aircraft's performance has also come under intense scrutiny, with some detractors assessing its manoeuvrability as mediocre and its weapons payload as inadequate. Its ability to counter the threat posed by increasingly sophisticated foreign types such as the Russian Sukhoi Su-57 and Chinese J20 has also been doubted.

It was reported in 2010 that the F-35 took 43 seconds longer to accelerate from Mach 0.8 to Mach 1.2 than the F-16 it is intended to replace. Concerns have also been raised about poor visibility from the F-35's cockpit,

LOCKHEED MARTIN F-35 LIGHTNING ▲

Lockheed Martin F-35 Lightning, 17-5251, 421st Fighter Squadron, Hill Air Force Base, Utah, 2019. Besides its internal carriage capacity, the Lightning II can carry external weapons/fuel tanks.

LOCKHEED MARTIN F-35A LIGHTNING ▼

Lockheed Martin F-35A Lightning, 15-5192, 34th Fighter Squadron, Al Dhafra Air Base, United Arab Emirates, 2019. During Operation Inherent Resolve, USAF F-35As made their combat debut. Several photos show them equipped with wing-mounted missile rails and with Luneberg radar reflectors.

gaps in its stealth coating, a fire risk arising from fuel tank vulnerability, engine problems, a high false alarm rate with the F-35's helmet, software failures and deficiencies and low availability and reliability.

In July 2015, a leaked Lockheed Martin report showed that the F-35 was less manoeuvrable than an older F-16D fitted with wing tanks. The Pentagon responded

that the F-35 was not intended for dogfighting but would instead disrupt enemy advanced air defences. It also has sensors capable of detecting and engaging enemy aircraft at beyond-visual-range, negating the need for close-in dogfighting. It has been noted,

too, that the F-35 may be able to offer greater manoeuvrability in the future.

Many earlier US fighters overcame developmental difficulties to become some of the best combat aircraft of their generation and it remains to be seen whether the same will be true of the F-35.●

▼ LOCKHEED MARTIN F-35 LIGHTNING

Lockheed Martin F-35 Lightning, 65th Aggressor Squadron, Nellis Air force Base, Nevada, 2022. In 2019, the USAF confirmed plans to reactivate the 65th Aggressor Squadron and equip it with F-35As. This image is a speculative demonstration of what these aircraft might look like.